Provincial Party Financing in Quebec

Harold M. Angell

University Press of America, Inc.
Lanham • New York • London

Copyright © 1996 by
University Press of America,® Inc.
4720 Boston Way
Lanham, Maryland 20706

3 Henrietta Street
London, WC2E 8LU England

Library of Congress Cataloging-in-Publication Data

Angell, Harold M.
Provincial party financing in Quebec / Harold M. Angell.
p.   cm.
Includes bibliographical references.
1. Campaign funds--Quebec (Province) 2. Political parties--Quebec
(Province).   I. Title.
JL258.A54   1995   95-39227 CIP

ISBN 0-7618-0156-1 (cloth: alk: ppr.)

DEDICATION

To my wife Sylvia, without whose support and assistance this book would never have seen the light.

TABLE OF CONTENTS

EPIGRAPH:

Commenting about politics while ignoring money is like talking about human anatomy without discussing the circulatory system.

T . B . Edsall

Politics is a rough business governed by opportunity and self interest more often than loyalty and duty. The 'best" governments and the "most honest administrations" are prone to abuse if not well scrutinized.

B.L. Vigod

TABLES

ix

INTRODUCTION

Party financing was not one of the things that began in French-Quebec in 1960, although in politics many things started then. Of course, some things that are now assumed to have impelled the Quiet Revolution must have begun before. For instance, there was the new ideology, called the "neo" or New Nationalism (French-Canadian). That is noted as a "prelude" to *The Quiet Revolution* by Michael D. Behiels, an historian[1].

Then there is the "class" which many scholars now assume to have been the motor force of the Quiet Revolution, as well as of the independence movement and the Parti Quebecois (PQ) in the late 1960s and 1970s. This class, sometimes called, in a full version, the new state technocratic middle class" is well documented. But Hubert Guindon seems to have been its discoverer and first describer in his QUEEN'S QUARTERLY article of 1964[2].

But in most things political, Quebec in 1960 must be called backward: in its electoral system, in its civil service, in its organization of government and of its legislative system. So, in many ways, the men of 1960 (there was no woman legislator until 1961) these men - Lesage, Levesque, Lapalme and Gerin-Lajoie were the more important - had to virtually create a modern system of government from scratch.

But that did not apply to party financing. That was well developed although they instituted a new system, involving a large amount of subsidy from the public treasury, in 1963. Before that it could be said that Quebec's system of party financing was "traditional". There had never been a party, particularly one in power, that did not acquire its party funds as a classical cadre party, if it could, with large contributions from the business world. This world, in Quebec, was still mainly "foreign" corporations (that is, any not French Canadian) mainly Anglo-Quebecer, other English Canadian, American or British - collectively, nearly all anglophone. Naturally, the party in power would get the lion's share of this manna. In addition, the party in power could "milk" its administration for party funds, in a way that would now be termed "corrupt".

As the sources for the study of the Duplessis regime's party financing system are rather more extensive than for the preceding Taschereau one, I feel on stronger ground in discussing its financing methods.[3] For the Taschereau system I have relied largely on Bernard Vigod's study[4].

WHY STUDY QUEBEC'S POLITICAL AND PARTY FINANCING SYSTEM?

The Quebec (provincial) party and political financing system is by now very different in many respects from those of the rest of Canada, although Quebec pioneered what is now the usual system in Canada, both federal and most provincial. This Quebec system, and the political effects it has had, is not well known or understood elsewhere in Canada or in the world. This does not seem to be due to the literature on it being mainly in French, for it is not. There was not much interest in the study of party financing in France until very recently[5].

In any case, the working language of the International Political Science Association (IPSA) Political Finance panel, in which most of the work has been presented, is English and my papers for it are in that language. Several have also appeared in French. In both languages they constitute - so far - , the main body of work on the Quebec party financing system. So there may be more interest in the Quebec system than one would expect for "just a province". As Louis Massicotte defines it, its system is certainly avant-garde[6], whatever may be thought of its intrinsic merits and the political effects it has had - and continues to have. It should interest, especially, students of political Science everywhere.

We suspected, 25 years ago, during the work for the federal Committee on Election Expenses, that there was more to party financing than met the eye. There were hints of its overriding importance in biographies and memoirs. The researchers for the federal committee, above all Khayyam Paltiel, its Research Director, and myself included, pulled together many of these hints and compiled a huge bibliography, quite apart from specific studies of party financing, mainly in Canada, in both the REPORT and in its accompanying volume STUDIES IN CANADIAN PARTY FINANCE (1966). These two volumes pointed the way and some of us - particularly Paltiel himself - followed it.

As far as the Quebec party financing system was concerned, hardly anyone reading about its avant-garde nature, either in the Canadian context or elsewhere, could possibly have foreseen the radical content of Bill 2 of 1977, from the QUEBEC ELECTION ACT of 1963. They could hardly have conceived the sweeping government subsidies for major parties by 1975 (and increased more than double in 1977).

The political effects of this new regime have been great, although somewhat unexpected. In the first place, the Quebec Liberal Party (QLP) was not destroyed by Bill 2's ban on corporate donations, as some expected. And the Parti Quebecois (PQ) was not the only party to profit. These quirks seem to have guaranteed the PQ's great fall in the provincial general election of December 2, 1985, and it had not sufficiently recovered (had it recovered at all?) by the next election on September 25, 1989 to perform much better. (The improvement in its performance was very slight).   In both elections it was deep in debt, while the Liberal party has been, in a colloquial phrase "rolling in Money".

We said back then, in the 1960's, that party financing was "the sinews of war", but we did not fully realise the implications. Louis Massicotte has shown[8] how the Quebec party financing, system has entrenched Quebec's two party system in its electoral law. The main factor lies in the original assistance to parties in 1963 - the partial reimbursement of candidates' election expenses.   But since the two major parties' candidates are guaranteed this reimbursement, and other parties' candidates must get 20 per cent of the vote to get it, the dice are loaded. Since most other assistance to parties is also only for major parties - those with seats in the Assembly - the dice are practically fixed.

Between the two present major parties (QLP & PQ) fortunes have swung from the PQ to the QLP since 1981, when the PQ was re-elected . If it has not always been the determining factor in this, party financing has always been an important indicator of possible electoral success.

The study of party financing in Quebec is important for the study of its whole political system, as well as for possible implications for other political systems -- and not only in Canada. The Quebec system remains avant-garde; whether it is also equitable is a different question.

The plan of this book is roughly chronological, in that it commences with the pre-Quiet Revolution situation. We consider the Taschereau and Duplessis party financing systems of parties in power. But the main focus of the book is from the beginning of the new party financing system from 1963. Thanks to this Election Act, we are provided with party and candidate reports of election spending from the 1966 election.

Apart from additional party subsidization to flesh-out the parties' "sucking at the public teat" as a colleague once described public subsidies, the next major topic is Bill 2 of 1977: "An Act to Govern the Financing of Political Parties".[9] The remainder of the book is a study of this legislation and the regime it established, reasons for it, and its effects to date, the most remarkable of which seems to be the QLP's adaptation into the system as a "Mass/Cadre" party.

There was a major amendment in April 1989.   The (Liberal) government raised the limit of an (individual - the only kind of contributions allowed) contribution from $3,000 per year aggregate to $3,000 per party per year.   This amendment could constitute a considerable breach in the wall raised by the PQ against the overwhelming power of money in Quebec politics.

This book is based on a number of papers and articles that I have written, principally over the past ten years. The first, "Political finance in Quebec" is the most comprehensive, and I have transplanted its title for this book's title.   It deals mostly with the party financing of the Duplessis Union Nationale regime.   But the book begins with a consideration of the party financing of the preceding Taschereau (Liberal) government.   This seems to be necessary as G. Martineau, Duplessis' Treasurer, was known to say often that "We took everything from 1935" that is, the last full year of the Taschereau regime.

Duverger[10] shows that it seems generally accepted that there are two main types of political party in western democracies from the viewpoint of their financing.   There is first the party based on the support of the business world for its financing; and second the party which gets most of its funds from mass support.   In Quebec, as increasingly in many parts of the world, there is a third type of financing, although not a third type of party, financing from government subsidy.

In the first type, that of the "cadre" or "bourgeois" party, according to Duverger [11] the method of financing may be centralized or decentralized, the latter normally being the older form.   In this latter case, candidates themselves or their local supporters may supply the bulk of their personal financing (for local election campaigns). The local committees are often richer than the central organization and are thus quite independent.   In the centralized type, on the contrary, those who supply the funds -- business, or people connected with business -- subsidize the centre.   As a result, it follows that when they have acquired this habit, the central organization of the party may exercise more pressure on the local groups.

Parties based on mass support may also be of two types. They may draw the bulk of their funds either from mass organizations which are affiliated to the party (such as, for example, the trade unions in the British Labour party) whose members are thus only indirectly affiliated to the party. In this type of party, funds may be supplied (often with a candidate attached) by such organizations. In addition to trade unions they may be cooperatives, etc. On the other hand, a party may be based on a direct mass membership, such as the French Socialist party, which pays its party dues regularly. The French Socialists (originally the S.F.I.O.) are interesting. Although at its origin it was based on the CGT union movement, (Confederation generale de travail) it lost this organizational support to the Communist Party (PCF). In Canada, the party which approaches nearest to a "mass" party at the federal level is the New Democratic Party (NDP). In fact, this party's predecessor (and co-founder), the Cooperative Commonwealth Federation (CCF) corresponded rather to the second type (direct) as concerned its financing, while the NDP leans increasingly to the first type (indirect) for its finances in its alliance with the Canadian Labour Congress (CLC). The differences seem largely the result of the requirements of a secure financial source, in addition to the CCF's severe financial distress and finally, to the Canadian labour and socialist tendency to follow British, rather than American, practices.

Until the appearance of the Parti Quebecois (PQ) in the late 1960's, Quebec had never had a "mass" party at the provincial level, neither from the viewpoint of membership nor that of financing (although the two *do* tend to go together.) The Ralliement des Creditistes was active only at the federal level in Quebec until 1970. Thus, the category of the "mass" party is relevant only for the period after 1960 although the Rassemblement pour l'independance nationale (RIN) (1960-68) was organizationally a small version. But it never won a seat in the Assembly.

These categories are useful it we are careful not to use them in too rigid a manner. It is obvious that certain parties cut across categories while others have several elements in their structures. And what are we to make of the new funding source in the past 30 years, government subsidization? No party in a democratic system is yet financed mainly this way -- although some Italian parties come close. But the point is, the identification of the *centre of gravity* in the financing of a party.

If this can be done through the analysis of parties according to these categories, it can cast light on the *true* nature of a party as distinct from its protestations -- even its constitution.

QUEBEC PARTIES BEFORE AND AFTER 1960

Before 1960:

Provincial parties which played a major role in Quebec before 1960 can all be put, at least provisionally, into the category of "cadre" or "bourgeois" parties. At least they were not - any of them - mass parties. They passed, historically, from a state of decentralization to a considerable degree of centralization. The first state corresponds with the period until around the turn of the century. In this period, the "parties" in the Legislative Assembly were essentially rather loose groupings created *within* the chamber by little groups of local notables, each one of whom was a powerful personage in his own locality[12]. This form of partisan organization was closely linked to the governmental instability which characterised Quebec during this period (until 1897).

A period of centralization at the provincial level followed, with the financial structure of the major parties having been essentially similar to those at the federal (central) level, that is, financing by the business world by means of a small number of relatively large contributions made to the party centre[13]. The party, as such, was an electoral "cadre" party and most of the funds were distributed for the local election campaigns and the "party workers" were mostly hired and paid workers at election time. The vast majority of the funds came from the most important companies -overwhelmingly English Canadian or American - which did business in Quebec, or from people closely linked to these companies[14]. Whitaker writes on this subject, "Before the Second World War, Montreal Liberals were closely associated with the great industrial, financial and commercial interests of that city. Although St. James street had no profound attachment to the Liberals, as such, and while some elements (such as Lord Atholstan of *The Star* and the CPR owners) might be more inclined to the Conservatives....Moreover, almost all the prominent French-speaking Liberal members from Montreal and its immediate surroundings were, themselves, closely associated with the large capitalist interests"[15]. Palatiel concludes, on this subject of the nature of the Canadian and Quebec parties: "The most obvious generalization to be made about the finances of Canada's two older parties (Liberal and Conservative) is that they look almost exclusively to business for the supply of their campaign funds. Both the Liberals and the Conservatives have tried with varying degrees of enthusiasm to widen their bases of financial support. To date (1970) these efforts have been a failure[16]. But the date *is* extremely important, for in 1974 the federal Election Expenses Act was passed, giving tax breaks for small contributions for the first time. Since then, the two old parties have tended to raise about as much from small contributions as they do from the traditional corporate donations. However, the PC Canada Fund's direct mail system has been (until 1990) overwhelmingly more successful than the Liberal corresponding effort".

PART I—PRE QUIET REVOLUTION

CHAPTER ONE - TASCHEREAU

With the rapid industrialization of Quebec, following the development of hydro-electric power as a basis, the political parties in Quebec were quickly being transformed from decentralized cadre (bourgeois) methods of party financing to more centralized method[17].

In the period at which we begin to examine Quebec's party financing, this process of centralization was under way, and so we will come across examples of both types of cadre party financing: centralized and decentralized. By the Duplessis era, the decentralized type - the candidate who finances his own campaign, from his own funds or from those of local backers, is the exception rather than the rule.

So, at the opening of the Taschereau premiership in 1920, we find two major decentralized cadre parties - with most of their funds raised by their candidates from local notables. Laurier's fund-raiser Israel Tarte is well known for his saying "Les elections ne se font pas avec des prières." His saying came at the close of an era when elections were mostly "a matter of prayer," as much within the Parti Bleu (Conservatives) as between them and Les Rouges (Liberals). Tarte raised funds for the Liberal party, and this meant the provincial Liberals as well as the federal ones in Quebec[18].

The new era of centralized fund-raising opened with the multiplication of the sources of donations after the turn of the century with industrialization. The two largest hydro companies - Montreal Light, Heat & Power and the Shawinigan company were great movers and shakers in Quebec's politics until the Montreal company was nationalized by the Godbout (Liberal) government in 1944 and Shawinigan was swallowed up, with the rest of the private companies, in the great Lesage (Liberal) nationalization of 1962.

There is a saying among those old enough to remember both, that Taschereau was "Duplessis with manners." From a reading of Bernard Vigod's book[19], it seems as if Duplessis built up Taschereau's cottage industry of party financing into a metropolitan venture. Taschereau's regime used money to buy influence in ways both legal and nefarious. But Duplessis changed the scale of operations.

Gerald Martineau, Duplessis' Treasurer, often said that their (Union Nationale) methods were "taken from 1935", that is, from Taschereau. Vigod feels that most of Duplessis' complimentary references to Taschereau were really self-serving attempts to justify his own political practices - that he had learned them from the master. Either way, the methods were basically the same but the scale was raised considerably. The Duplessis regime also seems to have used political violence to a considerably greater extent.

What was Taschereau's popular image? According to Vigod it was largely the creation of his political opponents. A "corrupt, reactionary regime" tied to "foreign" financiers.   The state of the QUEBEC ELECTION ACT was deplorable. Yet Taschereau defended his position openly and won four general elections despite an unfavorable economic climate during much of his mandate[20].

Could there be a better description of the Duplessis regime? Except that he won *five* general elections. Among historians of Quebec, there is something called "the Duplessis Archetype Syndrome"[21]. This is that the characteristics of Duplessis and his regime are essentially the same as those of his Liberal predecessors, for example, the theses of "Le roi negre" and the longevity of regimes. This, Vigod argues, is given general application to earlier leaders and governments, without investigation of different circumstances[22].

Thus, if we were to base our judgement only on this syndrome, it would be just as wrong to assume that kickbacks were the key to Taschereau's approval of resource development projects as it would be to ignore the realities of party financing and the blatant conflicts of interest he permitted[23].   However, we know about these practices only due to Duplessis' attacks on them before the Public Accounts Committee in 1935-36. But we don't know much about the party financing practices of the Duplessis regime, apart from the Report of the Salvas Commission in 1963 (See Chapter 2).

In Taschereau's political beginnings, there was enough and to spare of the financial practices later revealed.   As Vigod comments[24], "Taschereau accepted S.N. Parent's vision of an industrial future for Quebec.   He also assented, without much question, to Parent's assumptions that private gain by public officials and their associates was compatible with good government[25].

In Vigod's book there is seldom much direct reference to kickbacks on contracts or other practices which today would be accounted as corrupt. Yet there are hints. For example, as Taschereau joins the cabinet on October 17, 1907 as Minister of Public Works & Labour, Vigod comments drily: "This portfolio possessed some advantages - Public Works assured Parentistes (Taschereau's group) of fair access to the pork barrel[26].

As Taschereau became Quebec's 14th premier on July 9, 1920, there was one of his ministers, Walter Mitchell, in a nationalist caricature as "watchdog of St. James street[27]. In his first session the Taschereau government's most important bill for the Bureau of Public Charities was seen as almost inevitably becoming subject to the same partisan and personal chicanery which pervaded other state bureaucracies[28].

Even more than the ministers, their relatives and friends could grow fat on government and government-party business. Emile Moreau became a minor power in the Lake St. Jean region through his responsibility for party organization and patronage there[29].

COLLECTIVE PATRONAGE

In 1922 Leonide Perron (a Liberal minister) followed Arthur Sauvé (the Conservative leader) around the province promising new roads wherever he thought the opposition was making headway[30].

The Taschereau government's huge coup in this area was to take over the liquor business with the creation of its Quebec Liquor Commission (QLC) in 1921. Sauvé denounced this new bureaucracy as a new source of Liberal patronage. But something peculiar was happening. Liberal organizers were complaining bitterly at the lack of "cooperation" they were receiving from its Chairman, Georges Simard. Within a year or two, however, the chairman was changed and then the QLC quickly became the pool of government-party patronage it was to be for long after Taschereau retired.

ELECTIONEERING

Formal riding associations did not exist in the 1920s. Most deputies had personal patronage networks which served for electioneering purposes. The lack of local agents could spell disaster[31]. Nevertheless, more provincial road building was taking place - financed by revenue from the QLC[32]. Perron's road building came under fire for partisan administration in the 1923 general election[33].

Although the 1923 election saw heavy government losses (13 of the 15 Montreal seats) Taschereau put the return of his government down to the "eternal good sense" of rural voters[34]. The QLC "problem" was "resolved" when Simard agreed to resign in favor of a more cooperative party loyalist[35].

We may note that the rural voters generally had the same good sense in returning the government that Taschereau credited them with and that they kept it throughout the Duplessis regime. The phenomenon seems to have had a lot to do with the skewed electoral map, which became a lot more skewed by 1972, when it was finally reformed. The point was that a party could get many more seats for the same percentage of the vote - if they were the tiny population rural seats[36].

It is obvious that Duplessis was even more interested in the map's "skewness" than was Taschereau. And we have seen that Taschereau was *very* interested in it indeed.

The skewness of an electoral map refers to the distribution of its riding boundaries. They may be, like Quebec's before 1972, grossly out of line with the distribution of the population. Skewness is usually present when some ridings have several times the population of others. Quebec's map qualified, and also nearly all rural ridings had much smaller populations than the urban ones. Nevertheless, every riding elected a single deputy.

The disparity shows in the basic numbers (votes and seats) of the 1927 election[37]. The overall disparity then is that the Conservatives had 24.8 points less of seats than they had of votes. The Liberals had a big 25.5 points more[38]. A skewed map will return such a result more consistently.

The difficulties facing an opposition party (especially if the party is in opposition at both federal and provincial levels) are shown by Conservative leader Arthur Sauvé's troubles in the 1926 federal election. The federal and provincial Quebec Conservative factions were now united, but Sauvé was on the outside. The implications (for Sauvé) meant little financial support or good candidates for the expected 1927 provincial campaign. Sauvé said: "St. James street and *THE GAZETTE* had deserted him as part of a corrupt bargain with Taschereau. He (Taschereau) had continued to favour vested and foreign interests[39]. Sauvé had become nationalist. St. James street and *THE GAZETTE* could hardly be expected to continue to feed the mouth that bit them. If the provincial Conservatives did project an image that was consistent in 1926 and 1 927, it was of a party that rejected industrialization[40]. Duplessis, especially after 1944, projected no such image. In the iron ore dispute during the 1952 and 1956 election campaigns, Duplessis ever denied accepting much lower royalties than Newfoundland for essentially the same ore. In the 1956 campaign he spoke rather about all the benefits the province had gained from this developmant.

RELATIONS WITH TRADE UNIONS

Concerning these two premiers' relations with unions, for example Taschereau kept the alliance of the international (nonconfessional) labour movement. They supported Taschereau even more openly than the CTCC (Catholic) backed Sauvé, ignoring opposition attempts to exploit Taschereau's delay in proclaiming the new *COMPENSATION ACT*; evidently they agreed that "progress" was the issue[41].

In the countryside in the 1927 provincial election, the presence of immediate government patronage proved more attractive than the long-term reforms advocated by the UCC (Union Catholique des cultivateurs) allied to the opposition[42].

THE TASCHEREAU SYSTEM

Vigod describes the Taschereau system for staying in power as follows: Politically, Edouard Garon's (Minister of Agriculture) patronage system, along with Perron's road-building program and Perrault's colonization grants, was still delivering a solid bloc of rural Liberal deputies, whereas proposals of his critics contained major financial implications for the government[43].

TASCHEREAU'S PARTY FINANCING

Almost certainly the largest amounts in the Liberal party funds during Taschereau's premiership were from the "foreign" corporations, many of which were attracted to his province either by him personally, or by the conditions of doing business that he made sure to maintain. Vigod shows often that the Premier was always on excellent terms with these corporations. He shows it explicitly as well as implicitly. To document this point would be redundant—the whole book is redolent of it.

Critics then and later charged that Taschereau virtually "gave away Quebec's natural resources during the 1920s. To some extent this was obviously a Nationalist argument. The real objection was to "foreign" (that is, any non-French Canadian) ownership per se, not the terms on which resources were developed. Taschereau rejected this argument. It would be, he said, irresponsible to delay development until some hypothetical future time when French-Canadian entrepreneurs had attitudes, skills and capital to bring it about themselves[44].

The resource issue is also the most fertile ground to Fischer[45] and his "furtive fallacy", with campaign contributions the motive for concessions to the foreign entrepreneurs. But Vigod comments that there is little evidence for such an interpretation of Taschereau's policies. "Contracts were negotiated like businessmen", he writes, "without discussing the terms and giving formal sanction when necessary. The practice of retaining close friends of the government was neither unique to Quebec nor very "furtive" at all. But campaign contributions by these companies were similarly part of a common system, and in the Quebec Liberals' case there (was) a single fund for both federal and provincial elections, raised by designated bagmen who were closer to Ottawa than to Quebec City — Senator Raymond being the prime example[46].

But Vigod continues: "Where Taschereau actively contributed to suspicion was in so openly retaining discretionary authority instead of having agencies and procedures to regulate corporate behaviour in accordance with these policies[47].

Vigod next addresses the idea that, "Legitimate questions remain about the terms under which resource development occurred. While the profits and privileges enjoyed by some companies certainly reflected little credit upon the Taschereau government, it is easy to slip into a judgement of its conduct more appropriate to our own era than the earlier one"[48].

Yet the questions Vigod addresses in this passage are all governmental and administrative ones. He nowhere even broaches the questions of personal bribery or party fund contributions which might have been given in exchange for the grant of contracts, charges such as were rife at the time, at least among the Nationalist opposition.

Yet earlier we have quoted Vigod as saying: "Campaign contributions by these (resource) companies were similarly part of a common system[49]." Vigod says that: "The case of Montreal Light, Heat and Power is the most frequently cited in contentions that Taschereau allowed Quebec's resources to be exploited solely for the enrichment of a small corporate elite, and it is indeed impossible to justify the enormous profits of Sir Herbert Holt's enterprise.[50]" By the mid-1920s, Taschereau had apparently concluded that MLHP was an obstacle to progress in Montreal. But Taschereau "felt himself limited to ... indirect and ultimately futile means[51]."

Did Holt contribute to Liberal funds? Yes, handsomely. We know this, not from Vigod[52], who simply calls him a "Conservative financier"[53] but from other sources, such as Whitaker[54] where we find him (Holt) wheeling and dealing with Ontario Liberal Premier Mitchell Hepburn in the Beauharnois syndicate.

The great unanswered question of Taschereau studies, and it is exactly apposite to our topic, is: Was Taschereau personally or was his government involved in the Beauharnois scandal of the early 1930s? Vigod tells us that "in the 1931 election, the Liberals poured enormous amounts of money into relief projects during the three-week campaign[55].

What does Vigod mean by "enormous"? Surely he means more than usual, and we know from his accounts[56] that the Taschereau campaigns were well-oiled. But "enormous" is on a greater scale.

Although it was the federal Liberals who were mainly involved, there can be little doubt that the Taschereau government was also involved in these dealings. On the political side Regehr[57] concludes that the (Beauharnois) scandal typified the relationship between Canadian parties and their corporate benefactors. Certainly there was nothing unusual about the company having access to (Prime Minister) Mackenzie King through a Senator, who was also Chairman of the (company's) Board.

According to Regehr, the Special Select Committee was reluctant to conduct a broad investigation into the general area of election financing for fear of what would be revealed. The Committee did hear allegations of large sums having been paid, and there were allegations of other gifts to the ruling provincial parties in Ontario (Conservative) and Quebec (Liberal). The very size of the donation to the federal Liberals ($700,000) was extraordinary. According to Whitaker, it was more than the party could collect on Bay Street in two elections[59].

CONCLUSION (CHAPTER ONE)

Louis-Alexandre Taschereau has generally had a bad press since he was overthrown by Duplessis in 1936. Yet Vigod's biography is rather easy on him, to my mind. He writes that (Taschereau) showed a "coherent vision of French Canadian society, a liberal one which welcomed material and intellectual progress and rejected the isolationism and resistance to change favoured by traditional nationalist and ultramontane thinkers." He gives him credit for his courageous attempt to guide Quebec through the depression without ignoring a fatal inability to deal with issues of social security and the "electricity trust." He had, writes Vigod, a "genuine sense of public duty" and he fought in every federal and provincial election during his career[60].

Of course, he was anathema to the Nationalists. He said: "Whatever pretexts they might formulate, their anti-Imperialism sprang ultimately from a desire to discourage French Canadians from broadening their horizons, on the ground that the world beyond the St. Lawrence was irrelevant or hostile to their individual and collective aspirations[61].

So, Taschereau saw his political situation as a war between progress and stagnation, that is, industrialization versus traditional nationalism. The Conservative Armand Lavergne called Taschereau a Jingo and a traitor to his race[62].

There is little doubt that the Liberals in general, who spent 39 unbroken years in office in Quebec, and Taschereau's longevity in office in particular, was largely due to the party s financing system, which was mainly based, it seems apparent, on Taschereau's own extensive contacts in the business world, as well as those of two or three of his ministers and close associates. Taschereau had powerful and extremely wealthy opponents[63]. They dog him through Vigod's biography, namely "two powerful Montreal Conservative financiers, Rodolphe Forget and Herbert Holt." In 1911 we find Forget personally ousting Georges Parent in the federal election and "threatening unlimited financial support for opponents of Taschereau and Cannon in coming provincial elections".

Taschereau needed money, and lots of it. First there was the 1912 clash between Taschereau and the two financiers[64].   But Vigod recognised that the real significance of this affair was in the direct participation of Taschereau's close associates and relations to control municipal services and, more directly to our point, in the advent of formal links between the hydroelectric industry and the Liberal party leadership. In fact, Montreal entrepreneur F-A. Robert, for example, entered politics as a Liberal in 1912 in order to protect his growing interests[65].

Vigod also gives us a look at another aspect of Taschereau's close-woven system: that of his nepotism and cronyism[65 & 66].

Where did all the Liberal money come from? Taschereau established the Quebec Liquor Commission in 1921, virtually on taking office. Opposition leader Arthur Sauvé charged, in the 1923 election campaign, that Liquor Commission profits were financing the Liberal campaign,[67]. But, according to Vigod, the Liquor Commission was an electoral disaster[68].

But what is very hard to stomach, for anyone with a little knowledge of the period's politics, is what can only be called Vigod's apologia for Taschereau concerning the Beauharnois affair. At the beginning of his account (p.168) Vigod goes so far as to write: "But Taschereau was, if anything, slightly duped in the Affair", and "On the basis of no evidence whatever" Houde (an opponent) tried to implicate Taschereau. Yet "a number of federal Liberal politicians, including Mackenzie King, had accepted offered improper benefits" in connection with the Beauharnois project.

Could any politician with Taschereau's experience have failed to detect anything so big? In 1928, we are told, he had come to the support of a financially strengthened Beauharnois power syndicate, managed by R.O. Sweezey, an experienced engineer, well known in business circles. "All the improprieties occurred in the process of financing the venture and obtaining the necessary federal approval." "Moreover, none of Taschereau's political "friends" in Ottawa bothered to tell him when Herbert Holt insinuated himself into the Beauharnois organization[69]".

Vigod concludes the episode, in a footnote, "While there was (and is) no evidence to support Conservative accusations that the Beauharnois corporation "bought" his support in 1928, Taschereau did issue one explicit denial[70]. However, the French say "Qui s'excuse, s'accuse". Vigod continues: "His requests that King speed up the process of federal approval contain no hint of corruption, only genuine concern about the technical and financial problems created by further delay[71].

Really! Yet there was a pie of $700,000 to be cut up among the Liberal leaders. This was provided by an "unexpected stroke of fortune ,.. (in 1930) ... in the shape of Mr. R.O. Sweezey of the Beauharnois Power Corporation"[72].

But I have no doubt that Taschereau's most permanent stroke in the field of party financing was to establish the Quebec Liquor Commission in 1921. A knowledgeable politician, Israel Tarte, who had been Laurier's man-of-all-work, observed that it could be an embarrassment, as had been shown in other fields by the unhappy introduction of political patronage. That is what French Canadians feared above all.

The struggle against the establishment of a Ministry of Education was based on this very same fear. "Politics is going to seize our educational system. At least, that would be inevitable[73].

This was the judgement of one of the most celebrated Quebec journalists before World War I. She was essentially correct when, after a decade of debate, she singled out the main obstacle to the revival of a Ministry of Education.

So we must admire Taschereau's skill at politics all the more. He established his Quebec Liquor Commission early in his mandate. He was able to iron out most of the problems to its smooth running by the 1923 election. Ever since it has been a veritable gold mine for his successors.

CHAPTER TWO — DUPLESSIS

When Maurice Duplessis took power in Quebec in 1936, he found a full panoply of party financing—for the period. It is possible even that he knew more of its details than its creator, Taschereau, for Duplessis had investigated the system and had exposed much of it before the Legislature's Public Accounts Committee in 1935-36.

But it seems that Duplessis found Taschereau's cottage industry of party financing and developed it into a mercantile venture. Around this period (1935) Prime Minister Mackenzie King wrote in his *DIARY*[74] "that the question of campaign funds is the most baffling of all in connection with our electoral system". But we will see that, at least during his second mandate, from 1944-59, Duplessis solved this problem. What's more, not many Canadian provincial premiers have solved it as fully and as satisfactorily as Duplessis did. It was a time, moreover, before massive government subsidies to parties (which began in Quebec in 1963). So that one could say, without much doubt: "Tell me who finances your party and I will tell you what sort of party it is."

Our description -- of a cadre party funded by the province's business community -- seems valid at least for the Liberal party, which formed the opposition in the province from the end of the Second World War until 1960. It ruled before this from 1897. Let us not forget that from a federal viewpoint the Liberal party was a single organization -- organizationally the federal wing and the provincial wing formed a single unit until the initiative taken by Premier Jean Lesage to split them in 1964.

But can this description of the Quebec Liberal Party (QLP) from 1944-60 be applied to the provincial opposition party, the Conservatives, from the end of the First World War to 1936? Lacking categorical evidence on this point, we will simply give a few examples from the earlier period.

The Liberal party and the Conservatives (from 1936 the Union Nationale) are the two main parties in opposition of this century, certainly until the rise of the Parti Quebecois which replaced the Union Nationale in the 1970s. The two-party system was of the Liberals and the

Parti Quebecois from 1976. However, when we consider the major methods of party financing of parties *in power* during the whole of this period (end of World War I to 1960) in Quebec, we realize that they do not fall completely within our classification of "bourgeois" parties, at least as regards their major methods of financing. (They were certainly not "mass" parties either). What we have to deal with is a kind of party which consisted of an *electoral clique* which financed itself and maintained itself in power by the direct utilization of the administrative machinery of the state (or, rather, the province). This was done by a form of semi-official,"taxation," which directed considerable sums of money either to the campaign chest or directly to the branches of the party machine (even to individuals).

Our reference to "taxation" had, by 1960, two well-documented forms in this province. First there was the "sale" of licences and permits of all kinds — and above all liquor licences -which it was within the discretionary power of the provincial administration either to grant or withhold. To obtain one it was necessary to make a "contribution" to the funds of the party in power. To renew it annually a further contribution was required. During election campaigns, of course, it was necessary for licence-holders to "make an additional contribution" in order to prevent their licences being cancelled[75].

An example will show to what extent this system was rooted. A restaurateur recounted how, in December 1960, shortly after the change from a Union Nationale to a Liberal government, he paid $500 without question, necessary "to refill the government's campaign chest"[76]. Of course, it was a confidence trick. But the restaurateur paid without hesitation, fearing a refusal would cost him his liquor licence.

The second form, whose scale and institutionalization was fully demonstrated during the hearings of the Salvas Commission[77] after 1960, was the so-called system of "kickbacks" (in French "ristournes", in the U.S. often called "toll-gating"). In this system the prices of practically everything bought by the government was jacked-up above normal. The sellers understood very well that the difference between the normal sale price and the price paid by the government would be put at the disposal of the government party. Thus, during several months of inquiry the Commission heard hundreds of witnesses tell how several of the largest companies in Canada poured more than a million dollars into the Union Nationale's machine by this "kickback" method. They followed the directions of party people: MLAs, Legislative Councillors (upper house, abolished 1968), Cabinet ministers, and even the Premier himself. But the head of the system was "the great bagman" Gerry Martineau, the party Treasurer.

So entrenched and smooth-running was this system of "kickbacks" by 1960 that one is led to wonder why the Union Nationale found it necessary to accumulate the vast war-chest with which it was credited when the normal practice for paying organizers and workers was, apparently, simply to ask one of the companies which "owed" the government to send them a cheque. A random sample of the witnesses on a single day before the Salvas Commission showed five of them who received cheques from various companies. None of them had any connection at all with any of these companies. The only thing the witnesses had in common was that they had "worked for the Union Nationale."[78]

Now, there is no suggestion whatever that Duplessis somehow "gave up" the cadre party method of financing by large business donations. There is more than enough evidence that he never did. What is proposed is that the two semi-taxation methods (licences and kickbacks) were *supplementary* sources of party funds. Conrad Black, Duplessis' most admiring biographer, writes of him that: "
As the years passed that expertly tuned machine became hardly distinguishable from the State itself, going down to the grass roots to deal with the needs of voters, and up to the coffers of corporations anxious to get on with the unimpeded exploitation of Quebec's natural resources."[79]

In Black's main biography "*DUPLESSIS*", Mr. McConnell, owner of *THE MONTREAL STAR* and no mean industrialist, appears in the book's index 18 times. This is one measure of how close they were, There has never been any suggestion that Duplessis' party fund received fewer, or smaller business donations than, say, Taschereau. On the contrary a number of his policies indicate quite the opposite. (1) the major source of party donations was, collectively St. James Street (Rue Saint-Jacques). The Street had funded the Liberals for business reasons, but for a Conservative like Duplessis they gave wholeheartedly; (2) They were favorable to Duplessis' struggle against the federal government; (3) It is true that West-end Montreal switched its vote from Conservative to Liberal when the Conservatives became the Union Nationale in 1936 (and thus the more nationalist party), but the Street did not put its money where its vote was. The other features that the Street liked about Duplessis were his attitude to and treatment of labor in general and unions in particular. This, for them, was a gift from heaven. So, whatever he may have been to the rest of English Canada, Duplessis was a favourite to most of St. James Street. Duplessis had luck in this. Until 1941 the Street was run by a triumvirate: Sir Herbert Holt, the world's greatest hydro-electric magnate, President of the Royal Bank and Montreal Trust, Senator Lorne Webster and J.W. McConnell of *THE STAR*. The latter two were about as powerful as the first but, as we saw above, McConnell and Duplessis were very close. Then, in 1941, both Holt and Webster died on the same day, leaving McConnell in charge.

TAKEN FROM 1935: It was common parlance in Quebec that neither of these forms of party "self-financing" was *invented* by the Union Nationale. Martineau often repeated that he simply "took them from 1935" (the last year of Taschereau's Liberal regime). A striking piece of evidence is from the very first program of the Union Nationale in 1936. The first point of this platform reads (in part): "a law which will oblige all parties to publish the lists of their contributors.[80]

This must have been a very sore point back then. Andre Laurendeau (former editor of *LE DEVOIR*, Montreal) wrote on the subject of the Union Nationale's first convention in October 1961:

Taschereautisme in our view was the mark of a government ... whose influence was exercised everywhere because of patronage and which succeeded in getting reelected, notably because of an electoral machine in which the provincial police played a scandalous role ... in all these things, Maurice Duplessis hardly invented anything; he was the most faithful disciple of a premier whom he succeeded in defeating but whom he must have admired secretly.[81]

Apart from its financing practices, what the history of the Union Nationale demonstrates worthy of note is that under similar conditions a party need get its leaders elected only once. Once in power the government can separate itself almost completely from the party in whose name it took power. (An example here is the way Duplessis rid himself of Paul Gouin and the other leaders of the ALN (Action liberale nationale) which had actually elected more MLAs than the Conservatives in 1935).

The forms of financing which we have described made it possible for a Quebec government to finance itself as an electoral machine. The government controlled the party, which was very small in number — a cadre party of a few thousand workers — and, in a real sense, would "employ" this few. It would pay them off either in patronage of one kind or another or simply with straight cash. With the resources under its authority it could control them completely. Its financial situation was such that it could easily overcome any dissident element

LONGEVITY: This is the real explanation, we suggest, why the period of Liberal government lasted an incredible 39 years until 1936, and why Premier Duplessis could stay in power virtually a generation.

It is interesting to compare these two Quebec regimes to those which ruled before the era of modern administration, in Britain and the US, as well as in Canada. During a pre-modern era governments could practically always be sure of keeping power by the judicious use of patronage. In Britain, for example, during the whole of the eighteenth century the government of the day resigned only three times because of the loss of its majority in the House, and there is not one case where a general election resulted in the defeat of the government. This was, of course, before the Great Reform Act of 1832.[82]

Quebec was not an anachronism in this state of affairs. On the contrary a great deal of evidence could be cited that such situations were (even are) common in other provincial administrations and particularly in states of the U.S.

It seems that the methods developed for the financing of parties in power in Quebec were inherently extremely destructive of the spirit of democracy, and certainly more destructive than the methods classified by Duverger. This is because the Quebec methods made the parties much less amenable to any kind of control flowing from the financing structures themselves. Let us examine Duverger's parties from this point of view — mass first and then bourgeois.

MASS PARTIES: In parties which are financed directly by mass support, the leaders are much more subject to control, in spite of Roberto Michel's "Iron Law of Oligarchy" theory. Parties in this category (except Communist parties) are nearly always enthusiastic about democracy and its practices throughout their organization.

In order to maintain the membership dues and contributions rolling in regularly they *must* keep their supporters' interest and involve them in the life of the party. Financial controls are therefore semi-automatic; in the life of such parties if the supporters are unsatisfied they will certainly stop paying their dues and contributions — in fact, this is probably the first thing they will do. When enough of them do it the party faces a financial crisis — which inevitably leads to a crisis of conscience.[84]

In the indirect type of mass party (where the bulk of the funds comes from the affiliated unions, cooperatives, etc) the foci of power are multiple. Policy quarrels are often endemic,
as in the British Labour party between the union and constituency wings. Differences must be discussed in a fundamental way or the party may be threatened with splits. And as the bulk of the financing is controlled by the affiliated organizations, controls, again, are rather automatic.

In bourgeois-type parties, which are usually much less self-consciously "democratic", both in theory and practice, still there is implied, by their practices and structures of financing, much more control over their leaders than in the type of party we have described in Quebec — the government party before 1960 which can be called, for convenience, the "Administrative" party. By this term we mean parties in power in "pre-modern" systems of administration, which are self-financing as parties.

In the type of decentralized bourgeois party — in Quebec and in Canada the major parties before the turn of the century, (but there are modern examples) — there are as many foci of power as the party holds seats in the legislature. Each member (Commons, legislature) is head of a local clan and one wonders what local chief, who is the authority in his own area, will submit to the authority of his legislative leader? As long as his own seat is secure, and it is by definition, he can always threaten to join the opposition or to become an Independent. The party-group is held together by the hope of office, but in the final analysis the member is the strength of the party — he can permit himself the luxury of being free of the support of the party, because he owes it nothing, or very little, as regards his seat and local power. A typical example is represented by the classic Congressman or Senator in the United States who, so long as he carefully cultivates his local affairs in Washington, can permit himself a "deaf ear" when supposed "orders" come from the President. Extremes have been reached in Congress as it is less important than ever whether one is a Democrat or a Republican.

In the past several cycles all that seems to matter is to be an incumbent. Until 1994 almost all of these have been re-elected.

In the centralized bourgeois-type party, funds flow to the party from outside the organization. This money comes from organisms which are essentially impersonal and impelled primarily by the profit motive. They tend to aid any bourgeois party. Thus one finds, in Canada, the traditional 60/40 split of business contributions between the two major parties (Liberal and Conservative). The 60 share went to the government's party, of course.[86]

But the heads of the party must take account of the interests which finance them. This is a semi-automatic control little different —at least in theory — from those in effect in the more formal organizations of mass parties. The centralized bourgeois type of party is exactly the type generally thought to be applicable for Canada and for Quebec in particular.

It would be useful to give a pair of concrete examples of what is meant about controls being applied on centralized bourgeois parties through their financial structures. Example (1) Between the two Quebec provincial elections of 1923 and 1927, Arthur Sauvé, the opposition leader, achieved a reorientation of his provincial Conservatives towards an economic nationalism, which was coming into fashion in French Canadian intellectual circles at this period. On election day 1927, the (Montreal) *GAZETTE* (English), which had always supported the Conservative party, published a front-page editorial under the headline: "The issue outside Montreal is different — It is Liberal Versus Nationalist."[87]

THE GAZETTE was saying that Sauvé's provincial party was not worthy of the support of English-Canadian conservatives because of his French-Canadian nationalist leanings. (Nearly all political money in Quebec at that time was got from English-speaking companies). *THE GAZETTE* had clearly opposed Sauvé all through the election campaign, speaking in contemptuous fashion of the "Sauvé faction". As a result, Sauvé had great difficulty in collecting money for this campaign, and his Treasurer bitterly complained in Montreal, before the Conservative Club, about the paucity of the contributions.[88] That is an example of a control which is rapid and direct.

Now, a more recent example, from Canadian federal politics. A Liberal fund-raiser, James Scott, tells how he was sent to an important businessman who could not only refuse a large contribution from his own company but who could also influence other donors. The contribution was promised but "after two days he called me in anger because, in the meantime, our party had taken a position on a certain problem." This position, he said, showed that we were "on the unions side." The man tried his best, said Scott, to change our position. Scott's conclusion is "that all political parties have experiences like this from time to time with their contributors and it is very rare that the result is a significant change in policy."[89]

What should interest us most in Scott's story is the frank admission of the possibility of a party or a government's change of direction. Although Scott does not mention it, one also finds in this situation what is called the "law of anticipated reactions." In any case, the existence of pressures on party leaders is evident. The importance of this situation is shown by the sham played out by Canadian prime ministers since Mackenzie King in the Beauharnois scandal, when he pretended to be divorced from his party's fund-raising machinery. This shamming is too flimsy to be credible. The pressure is applied, and is effective, whether on policies, personnel decisions or administrative questions. This has been demonstrated. Clearly, there are controls flowing from the financial structure. However, it should go without saying that a small businessman with $50 to contribute to a party is not going to have the same access as will an executive of a large corporation with $50,000.

In Quebec, there was a set of evidence until 1960 for the essential difference between bourgeois-centralized parties according to whether they were the government party or the opposition. This was the rather high attrition rate for leaders of opposition parties as compared to almost nil for leaders of governmental (or "Administrative" parties). It is apparent that pressure could be applied successfully to topple opposition leaders. (This in a provincial party system in which leaders, at least theoretically, served until death or resignation and where there was no provision for leadership review. But did Quebec ever see, between 1904 and 1960, a *Premier* driven from office? The only example is Louis Alexandre Taschereau in 1936, and that took what can be termed a political earthquake after a split in his own tight little inner circle.[90]

We could multiply the examples of a drought of contributions imposed on a party by business. There is the famous case of Prime Minister Arthur Meighen in the 1921 federal election.

There is the case of federal Conservative leader Manion in the late 1930s. These are interesting but do not forward the argument. This argument is that there were *no controls* on the tight little circle of leaders of an "Administrative" party[91] neither within nor without, which could be derived from its financial structure. In this type of party the leader and a little oligarchic clique can have absolute control. These people, if they stick together, can almost completely self-finance and also self-perpetuate. Outside the "party" money is produced involuntarily, thanks to a system which can be compared to the public finance of the State itself, and authorized by similar sanctions (withdrawal of permits and contracts) as Duplessis did many times. For example, there is the Roncarelli case, decided by the Supreme Court in 1959.

Within the organization finances are from the top down, controlled completely by the oligarchy.

What forms of pressure remained (that is, non-financial)? Democracy? The electorate? With Bill 34 and its single enumerator whole cemeteries could vote — Union Nationale. In general. in such systems, the "machine" was well kept and well oiled.[92]

Still more was it looked after, particularly in Quebec in the period as in other similar systems, by a more than simply skewed electoral map.[93]

There remained only the possibility of a force from outside the provincial political system. Such was exerted by the *federal* Liberal government and party in Quebec in the provincial election of 1939 — a *provincial* election but with federal, even international stakes. The main question was Canada's war effort, opposed by Premier Duplessis. The main Liberal effort was to convince the Quebec electorate that a Duplessis victory would cause the mass resignation of all Quebec federal ministers, leaving the province defenceless against the imposition of conscription.

The other possibility of an outside force is what actually did happen — the natural death of a leader(s). So, in 1959-60 there was an internal crumbling and split in the leadership elite (Duplessis died in 1959 and his crown prince, Paul Sauvé, three months later). Only such an event from outside could break the grip of the leadership elite of the "Administrative" party.

One other feature of Duplessis' "Administrative" party regime should be noted, and that is its main policy of provincial autonomy. Duplessis could be a French Canadian nationalist --in his own terms —because he did *not,* like his predecessor as Conservative leader, Arthur Sauvé, depend on the business community for his funds. In fact, as we have learned, he could *force* them to supply him with funds in the form of kickbacks and contributions. They could *not* control him in any real way, Of course, they could do business with him because he was a convinced believer in capitalism and free business enterprise, as well as a conservative in social and especially in labour areas. But they still hated him, many of them, for his — mostly symbolic — French Canadian nationalism. But they could not control him, so when he was against the war, he was against the war.

SUMMARY

Before 1960, Quebec parties may be called "bourgeois." They passed from decentralization to a large degree of centralization. They were financed by business, by means of relatively large individual contributions given to the central organization of the party. Most of these funds were expended for local election campaigns and the parties were of the "cadre" type, according to Duverger's categories. The bulk of the general fund came from important companies in the province, the property above all of English Canadians or Americans. This description seems valid, at least for the opposition parties, from the end of the First World War to 1960.

However, the parties *in power* during this period do not correspond to this description, considering their main methods of financing. The Liberals under Taschereau (and perhaps also under Sir Lomer Gouin before him, but we have little evidence to verify this) as well as the Union Nationale under Duplessis, quickly became electoral cliques which were self-financing and maintained themselves in power by the direct use of the State's administrative machinery, through patronage, the exploitation of licences and kickbacks.

This "Administrative" party system was refined to a point where the essence for a party consisted in a single operation to permit its leader to take power. Once in power the government could separate itself almost completely from its nominal "party", if it wished, and the forms of financing gave the government the possibility of self-financing as an electoral machine. Taschereau ruled from 1920-193`6 and Duplessis from 1936-39 and from 1944-59, almost without problems in this area.

Finally, it is possible to say that the methods used for financing "Administrative" parties in Quebec were more destructive of the spirit of democracy than those classified by Duverger, because much less subject to any form of control. Parties financed by mass support *must* cultivate that support. The controls are thus semi-automatic. In bourgeois parties there are also controls on the leaders implicit in the financial practices. These leaders must take account of the interests which finance them and they may be subjected to sudden cut-offs (droughts) in financing.

The main argument of the first two chapters is therefore that there were no controls at all on the "Administrative" party flowing from its financial structures. Only pressures from outside the system could have effect, at least as long as the elite of such a party remained united.

PART II--1960, THE QUIET REVOLUTION AND AFTER

CHAPTER THREE--1963, BILL 15.
THE QUEBEC ELECTION ACT

The main Quiet Revolution in Quebec is usually dated from 1960, but our story takes up at 1963 with Bill 15, the new **QUEBEC ELECTION ACT**. I think enough time has passed that I can refer to myself as one of the principals in the making of this Act.[143]

What was involved, from a party financing point of view? For the first time in Quebec — or indeed in Canada — there was government subsidization of party funds. The method used was the partial reimbursement of qualified candidates' election expenses. Those qualified were those of any party — or none — who obtained at least 20 per cent of their riding's vote. Yet many more than these were qualified; for also qualified were all candidates whose party (or Independent) candidate had come first or second in the previous election. This meant that about double the number of a full slate of candidates were *guaranteed* reimbursement, regardless of how many votes (or none) they had obtained.

There were also a few small concessions to candidates, such as a number of copies of lists of voters. But there was nothing for parties as such. The main point was that a party's largest single expense, in those days, was its subsidy to its candidates. Few candidates would run at all without money from the party. So the reimbursement was very welcome where it was most needed. Money for the party as such comes later, but the ice was broken by Bill 15. Here for the first time in Canada was government money going directly to the party organizations. Also included was payment for party offices.

Why did the Lesage government feel the need for such radically new money? The previous year (1962) this government had been re-elected in a one-issue election — to nationalize the private hydro-electric companies. Now, St. James Street never liked any nationalization, from as far back as Meighen and the CNR (Canadian National Railway) in 1921. So we can imagine that Lesage's bagmen came up dry from their expeditions.

In addition, Lesage was planning the big organizational split that Lapalme had hungered after — between his party and the Feds — in 1964. Presumably Lesage would have no call on federal party funds. Short of being left in a situation like that of Lapalme, Lesage innovated for "new" money. It was expected of him, as a premier who had innovated so much already. Still, Lesage never won another election. The disaster of 1966 was too much for him. He retired in 1969, a year before the next election was due.

The first concentrated effort in Canada to discover some of the data of party financing was that of the Committee on Election Expenses.[144] The main text of this study details how Bill 15 was made. Added is a study of the law's effects in the 1966 election — its first.

Although there was no orderly set of data on party financing in Canada, we did find that, in former Quebec elections, it was indicated that provincial campaigns were more expensive than in any other province. This has apparently been true from the very beginning of democratic institutions in Quebec.

One problem with imposing an overall limit on party spending was the Union Nationale's custom of spending public funds for electoral purposes, such as the payment of hospital bills, gravel deliveries, road and bridge building, grants for schools and hospitals etc. None of these expenditures could be curbed by an overall party limit. A government need merely contend that these are not "campaign" expenditures at all, but simply public works for which the time was right. All governments use tactics like these in elections.

Whatever our hesitations, Bill 15 did fix an overall limit on both party and candidate spending. The Act still limits the spending for a party's campaign to a maximum of 25¢ per elector on the lists.[145] Had this provision been in force for the previous (1956) election, it would have imposed an absolute maximum of $693,196 for a party which had candidates in all ridings. But as to the circumstances which brought the legislation into being, whether the Union Nationale's spending in 1956 was reasonable or not, in terms of what happens somewhere else, was not the real issue: after Pierre Laporte's series of articles, the lid blew off. What lay at the basis of the agitation for reform? It seemed to me then as now, that it was not the fact that one party spent so much but the fact that the expenditure of the other party was so small that there could be no effective answer made to the government-party's propaganda. The Liberal party's campaign was overwhelmed. It was this disproportion in the intensity of the rival campaigns which gave the impression, as Laporte wrote, of a complete falsification of "le jeu normal de la democratie (the normal play of democracy)."[146]

Taking a minimal figure for the Union Nationale and a maximal figure for the Liberal party, we still have a disproportion in expenditures in 1956 of the order of eight to one. It was this disproportion more than anything else which aroused concern for the normal processes of democracy, and stirred up public support for the proposed legislation.

A. THE TRADITIONAL PATTERN

To ascertain what the traditional pattern had been in Quebec one could consult the Hamelins', *LES MOEURS EIECTORALES DANS LE QUEBEC.*[147] This work shows how, from the very earliest times (1770's), the cost of distributing liquor to the voters was always a large item of expenditure, and if the battle became tough the candidates were resigned to distributing cash. However, more or less successful attempts were made, in the nineteenth century, to reform the situation. From 1869 certain provisions of the United Kingdom *CORRUPT PRACTICES PREVENTION ACT* of 1854[148] were introduced. But the penalties were small fines and the amendments gave little in the way of results.

The Quebec legislators went further in 1875[149] in an attempt to correct this weakness. They required that every candidate was to make his payments only through an agent who had to make a detailed report of election expenses which might be published in the *OFFICIAL GAZETTE.* The public could examine the accounts and verifying documents of every candidate. In case of an incorrect report, there was imposed a fine of $500. But an amendment of 1892 freed candidates from the obligation of supplying a detailed account of their electoral expenses. Thus a return to unbridled corruption began, especially as the courts, in cases of election contestations, showed themselves indulgent.[150]

The reformist wing of the Conservative party took the *ELECTION ACT* in hand once more in 1895.[151] Once again, the law required each candidate to supply a detailed account of his expenses. Further, only an agent appointed by the candidate could make payments or loans during an election campaign, and, for the first time, not only had the agent to maintain a *DAILY* statement of election expenses, but the Act fixed a maximum of expenditures. Thus in 1895 the province could pride itself on possessing one of the most advanced election acts in the world.

But it did not last long and the same people who would amend it several years later lived to bitterly regret their actions.

The Act of 1875 marked the opening of the period which can be called "professional" in electioneering. From that time people's support had to be bought, and it was therefore necessary to organize the election fund in a rational manner. To draw from the public treasury seemed the easiest solution to hungry politicians, if an honest way could be found to make the transfer. This was accomplished by a system, by 1960 hallowed by tradition, popularly called "kickbacks" (tollgating or in French "ristournes"). Percentage on contracts, and commissions on the privileges and favours given by governments, resolved the technical difficulty. Politics became synonymous with scandal and we should add that not only Quebec was involved.

The novelty consisted not in the *use* of public funds for electoral purposes, but in the systematization of this breach of trust. Before 1875, brutality was the major method; after it both parties justifiably accused each other of dabbling with public funds for partisan ends. Scandal led to scandal. When power changed, the new government-party denounced the gluttony of its predecessor. These methods of financing campaigns naturally did not apply to the opposition party except as it could promise future contracts and favours. Apart from this it had to rely on relatively large donations from a small number of businessmen and industrialists.

Once the problem of raising funds was settled, it was necessary to organize their distribution. The advances of finances by the party treasurer, assisted by the party managers (organisateurs), considerably reduced the members' independence. It was a means of control by the party over the candidate; a means of keeping strong personalities on a leash or of eliminating undesirables.

THE TWENTIETH CENTURY

Until 1963 the law added to the numbers of voters. But it neglected the means of control of election expenditures. A few strokes of the pen were sufficient for a retrogression of 30 years. The widening of the suffrage contributed to a reorientation of electoral practices. In place of dealing solely with the individual, the parties became more interested in groups, and electoral practices became complex. In the manipulation of groups, capitalists were given forest limits, watercourses, permits for the exploitation of natural resources, and contracts. Natural resources were bartered for election funds. To the clergy, grants and privileges were exchanged for their neutrality, their photographs, their prestige, their influence and their smiles. Newspapers in Quebec have always needed subsidies. The party in power offered its millions, asking in return only silence. It was apparent, that the first Union Nationale victory in 1936 owed a great deal to radio propaganda, which pierced the wall of silence erected by a salaried press. Then the Union Nationale, in its turn, carried the system to its apogee, having learned much, as we saw, in Taschereau's school.

Now let us examine the period immediately preceding 1960. The Union Nationale had ruled uninterruptedly from 1944 and had perfected a remarkable election machine. What was the fuel that powered this machine? Where did it come from? And to what purposes was it put? Such an inquiry is necessary since any regulation of party funds involving publicity or limitations must needs take methods of financing into account.

In Duverger's categories[152] all Quebec provincial parties until 1968, with the foundation of the Parti Québecois (with the possible exception of the Créditistes[153]) were "middle class" or "bourgeois" parties. They were financed by the business community. They became centralized after the turn of the century. In this period the financial structure of Quebec's major parties seems to have been essentially the same as for the Quebec parties in the federal arena, that is, business-financed by large companies making large contributions to the centre (bagman method). The money was then distributed to the local candidates. Most of the general fund came from the most important companies operating in the province. There were varying numbers of notables in more or less firm control of their ridings or regions and thus less amenable to control by the provincial leadership than they would have been if they had been more dependent on it for funds. This description seems to be a fair one, at least of the opposition party in Quebec from about the First World War to the 1960's.

In mass parties, such as the Parti Québecois, the financial control is the strictest one which the members hold over the leaders and the central organization.[157]   Within a bourgeois party financial controls can be sudden and cut sharply, as we saw in the cases mentioned — Meighen in 1921, when St. James Street felt he had nationalized the CNR; Arthur Sauvé, Quebec Provincial Conservative, in 1927. His turn to nationalism left his campaign without funds. There are other examples. The point is, that these are controls -- real controls.   They are not always democratic controls, but they are certainly controls.

The central point is that no controls at all are exerted on the leadership circle in an "Administrative" party deriving from its financial structure.

LA REFORME ELECTORALE: PREPARING THE PARTY AND THE PUBLIC

Between the Lesage Liberal election victory of 1960 and the new *QUEBEC ELECTION ACT* in 1963 there were many in the party, and not a few, who expected to slip comfortably into the role of the former Union Nationale. They were disappointed by the civil service reforms, which were virtually the first carried out by the new Quebec government. By this means the scope of patronage was greatly diminished.

The question then was: what specific electoral or related reforms would be appropriate? There were several possibilities: publicity, limits, subsidization. If subsidization, which it seemed this government would choose, what kind of subsidy? A grant to parties? Reimbursement of election expenses (central campaigns, or candidates' election expenditures?).

The Quebec Liberal Party, in its platform for the 1960 election, stated in Article 48 "election expenditures will be limited."   In its first convention after the election it resolved that, since electoral reform could not be effective without a limit on election expenditures, they should be limited according to reasonable standards.

In elaboration of the party's program and in preparation for the following convention in November 1961, which had "Electoral Reform" as its theme, the Political Committee (La Commission politique) of the Federation (QLF — Quebec Liberal Federation) prepared a study paper for circulation to the regional conventions. This took place during the summer of 1961. This document summarized the thinking of the leadership on the question of political finance and its dangers.

One third of the questionnaire was concerned with the financing of candidates and political parties and the control of election expenditures. The questions show the lines along which the party was being guided. There was a question which dealt with the reinstatement of the position of "Election Agent." Of the remainder, the most important were whether the province should reimburse candidates and/or parties for election expenses, and if so — what criteria should govern such payments: a minimum of votes? or a minimum of members elected? If the principle of reimbursement were accepted what specific expenses should be covered, or should an overall sum be given? Should there be *limitations* on the electoral expenses of candidates and parties? How might these be enforced? Should *contributions* to political parties be limited or controlled, and if so how? Should the province contribute to the expenses of parties outside campaign periods? Altogether the questions were detailed and advanced in tone. Some were implemented in the new *QUEBEC ELECTION ACT*, many not, but this writer felt that they were not lost sight of by the Federation and would well come up again, especially after at least one test of the Act in an election. In any case, as we will see, the most important document, by the Parti Québecois, another party entirely, was Bill 2 of 1977. It built on Bill 15 and did not cancel any of it.

Public opinion was running for party financing reform. This is shown by the fact that in the early 1960's a good number of Unionistes were thinking along these lines. The party's first leadership convention, indeed its first convention of any kind, was to be held in October 1961. A leading candidate, Jean-Jacques Bertrand, proposed that party political funds should be controlled by a trust company and he pledged his support for legislation limiting election expenses.

REPORT ON ELECTORAL REFORM IN QUEBEC

During the summer of 1961 this writer was commissioned by Mr. Maurice Sauvé, then Campaign Director of the QLF, to make a survey of legislation and practices on political financing in Canada and other appropriate countries in order to recommend those which seemed suitable for adoption in Quebec. What were considered were: the limitation of campaign expenses, publicity of campaign funds. T h e study was submitted in September, published by the Federation in October and distributed to the delegates to the convention which was held November 10-12, 1961 in Quebec City. It was the source of a number of resolutions, some of which were in Bill 15 the following year.

OFFICIAL AGENT

On experience in the United Kingdom I considered the reinstitution of a candidate's official agent as the most important step. It is easier to prosecute for technical offenses than for substantive ones. Under the system of official electoral agents it becomes an offence for anyone to spend money locally in support of the candidate except through the agent, and for the agent to spend any money for which he does not account, or spend money above the permitted amount. Thus, it is necessary only to prove that money has been spent, not that it has been spent corruptly. Therefore the establishment of the post of official election agent, with all its necessary implications, was seen as the prime prerequisite for an effective system of limitation and control of candidate expenditure.

PAY FOR VOTES

It is possible to pay voters for assistance other than assistance by their votes. It is difficult to strike at this directly, as is demonstrated by the *CANADA ELECTIONS ACT* and several provincial Acts. Even the old *QUEBEC ELECTION ACT* had such a useless provision. It is obvious that if anyone ever took such provisions seriously, the only prospect would be endless litigation. Thus, limitation through a specified allowance for election expenditure would be much simpler and more effective. For the limitation of campaign expenses of parties, the argument against the idea of the overall limit, and for the more direct attack by way of publicity, seemed to hold good when applied to the provincial situation.

RAISING FUNDS

Whatever controls might be put upon sources of contributions, tradition, custom and the very climate of Canadian politics would seem to make it inevitable that the party in power would find it easier to obtain money than any opposition. Thus the main problem would seem to be that of ensuring that opposition parties would have available to them funds and facilities more equal to those of the party in power. This presents a strong argument for some form of state assistance for party campaign funds. If means could be found to level up the resources of the opposition with those of the government-party, much of the bitterness might be removed from the discussion of election laws, and the practical consequences of major shortcomings of these laws would be greatly reduced.

We discussed two alternatives to such controls: one to limit the amount which any individual or firm might contribute to a party organization,the other to require the publication of party accounts. We will see that both were instituted in Quebec in Bill 2 in 1977. The idea of publicity seemed more promising. Its advantage is that, once established, it is to some extent
self-enforcing because if accounts of some sort, in some official form, are published by all parties, the matter is thrown open to debate.

In addition, as we saw, the problem for Quebec was rather one of levelling up party expenditure than of directly controlling and limiting it. Thus direct control by way of a general limit to be imposed on the amount any party could expend from its central fund on an election campaign was not recommended. However, it was recommended that the possibility should be investigated of imposing limitations on specific types of campaign expenditures, which might be a more practicable and manageable proposition.

Specific suggestions for reforms in reporting of candidate financing are not common in Canada, in spite of the obvious and notorious inadequacies of the federal Act until 1974. This writer felt the auditing of statements to be a commonsense, practicable proposal which is well supported by writers on the subject in other countries; it is based on normal business methods. The common complaint that the campaign funds declared under Sec. 63 of the *CANADA ELECTIONS ACT* usually were, until 1974, a formality, with nominal amounts entered under the appropriate heading, could be simply met by an independent audit of accounts which would serve to prevent such problems. This type of audit was therefore recommended.

It would have been perfectly feasible to base an effective reporting system on an adaptation of the *CANADA ELECTIONS ACT* (until the federal *ELECTION EXPENSES ACT* of 1974 of course). However, the notorious flaws would not have been incorporated, especially that which permitted candidates to be excused for their failure to report. The additions needed were in the receipt and auditing of reports, the enforcement of provisions for agents, the imposition of penalties on candidates, and the summarization and publication of the reports.[158]

In my *REPORT ON ELECTORAL REFORM IN QUEBEC*[159] the main recommendations to achieve these ends were those which envisaged either the establishment of an independent commission or the broadening of the responsibilities of the CEO (Chief Electoral Officer) and his staff to receive, audit, summarize, publish and preserve the reports and the information they contain. (These functions are presently (1995) performed by or under the direction of the DGE (Directeur général des élections). Exposure of political funds to public view need not involve the imposition of complicated restrictions which invite evasion. What was needed was an effective pattern of public reporting which would promote public confidence in the party and electoral machinery, and contribute toward a more informed and enlightened electorate, without impeding free participation.

There are many different forms of party financing, actual and potential. Several methods, well known elsewhere, have not been tried in Canada to any extent. This indicated the need above all to allow flexibility in the administration of a publicity system. The achievement of this objective was most capable of fulfilment if it were made the responsibility of an administrative body, which would maintain flexibility in the regulations and recommend changes in them to keep them up to developments in the area.

The effectiveness of a publicity system depends largely upon the conscientious fulfilment of the duties assigned to the repository. (In our present case it is the DGE). It is an important question whether the publicity requirements imposed on political parties should cover only campaign finances or whether annual reports should be required. It seemed reasonable (if the province were to be asked to undertake any considerable subsidy of the operations of parties) to require annual reports rather than merely reporting of campaign finances.

Another recommendation was that an interim report be required of the treasurer of every association of candidates (definition of political party) preceding polling day. These reports would be filed not later than the third day following the effective reporting date, thus allowing at least one week for publicity before the election. The final reports of the parties' receipts and expenditures in connection with the campaign would then be required within three months following polling day.

It was shown that by far the major "above board" expenditure in the election campaign is that which comes under the heading of "publicity."[160] It seemed that in the future it would also likely take up a growing portion of campaign budgets. I recommended, therefore, that the prescribed forms should stress the detailed reporting by parties of expenditures of this type. In the case of restrictions being enacted these reports would provide a check as to compliance. Details should be required of space bought in newspapers,and time bought on radio and television stations.

The emphasis throughout the Report was on the cleansing power of disclosure and attendant publicity, and upon the encouragement of openness and wide circulation of information. As distasteful as disclosure might be to those involved (and every attempt should be made to protect the privacy of the individual) yet organizations and groups must be prepared to defend their motives publicly. There can hardly be an alternative to this in a democracy.

After a survey of possible methods, it was clear that there were various ways in which governments can help to finance political activities. The choice of method deeply involves political questions rather than merely technical ones. The point stressed was that one could not hope to offer any "best" solution to the problem, but only to propose the various alternatives along which choices might be made by the politicians.

We looked at a tax-benefit for contributions scheme, with some or all of the specific and direct subsidies to candidates that were possible. This could do much to accomplish the aims of the Quebec Liberal Party. On this basis, although detailed recommendations did not seem to be in order, the following general ones were considered appropriate:

(1) That there should be no subsidies to parties as such,   except perhaps (a) in the form of tax-supported contributions from private individuals:

(b) in the form of arrangements for the provision of free broadcasting time on commercial radio and television stations.

(2) That there should be direct subsidies of certain specific expenses for candidates.

All parts of the report were closely interconnected. To note only a few of the major points: if the State were to take over any considerable part of the costs of elections, then it might well be necessary to reduce the maximum permissible expenditure of candidates; if it is possible to arrange for free broadcasting time on commercial radio and television, then this would affect the suggested maxima on time which might be bought by the parties, or it might be possible to eliminate the possibility of their buying time altogether. The information which would be brought to light and analyzed by the Registry would almost certainly necessitate the review of the treatment of the other subjects even after only one election. However, at this time no one anticipated a snap election, like that of November 1962. There seemed to be another aspect of interconnectedness too. It was that if the State were to provide assistance in any or all of the various forms suggested in a way that appeared to them to be impartial, then it would be likely that politicians would take more kindly to the regulation of maxima on spending and the requirements on reporting.   If aid were to be provided, then there would be more justification for what might appear to many to be interference and inquisitiveness.

PRESS REACTION

From press releases at the end of August 1961, both *THE MONTREAL STAR* and *LE DEVOIR* commented on the Report in editorials (in *LE DEVOIR* signed by Pierre Laporte). They announced that it would be distributed to the delegates to the QLF convention in November. When the Report was released at the beginning of November, comment was widespread and reaction was generally favorable. *LA PRESSE* gave it the most elaborate treatment, with four long articles by Guy Lamarche appearing on successive days from November 7-10. *THE STAR* reported on it and commented editorially on November 11.

QUEBEC LIBERAL FEDERATION CONVENTION, NOVEMBER 10-12, 1961

Response and interest were lively in the work of the convention. 243 resolutions on electoral reform were submitted before the meeting, not all on party financing, but more were expected from the floor.

The big guns were at full blast on electoral reform right from the start. It was pushed, or at least mentioned, by all the opening speakers: by Mr. Francois Robert, the outgoing President, by Premier Lesage, the leader, and by Dr. Roger Brault, the Secretary, who was later elected the new President.

Premier Lesage said that much remained to be done. They had chosen "Electoral Reform" as this convention's theme. "That is one of the major measures we must realize in the session which begins in January," and there was no doubt that their deliberations would produce much of great use to the government in the preparation of its legislation.

In his report on the activities of the Political Committee (Commission politique) Mr. Alphonse Barbeau, the co-Chairman (President-adjoint) said that they had paid particular attention to the question of electoral reform. The committee on the annual theme had been composed of Messrs. Guy Favreau and Jerome Choquette and Mrs. Yvette Dussault-Mailloux. The Committee, inspired by the resolutions received after the questionnaire, had prepared an edition of the resolutions. This served as a basis for discussions during the convention in the three committees established to discuss electoral reform. The Commission had concluded that while it was opportune to approve the granting of subsidies to political parties, it felt that it was not then opportune to take a stand on two other questions referred to it by the 6th Convention: political parties to make public reports on the origin, amount and usage of their funds, and the deduction for tax purposes of contributions. (Both of these are in effect now in Quebec, but they had to wait until Bill 2 in 1977 to be enacted).

TRADITIONAL POLITICS

Discussion of electoral reform was very brisk and sometimes heated at the Convention, in its committees and plenary sessions. However, as the newspapers reported, most of the delegates seemed more interested in discussing patronage. Those opposed to electoral reform took the line that the party was adopting such a highminded approach that it might suffer at the polls. The delegates were genuinely concerned about the possibility that, as *THE STAR* put it, the reforms might "become a collective headstone to a number of Liberals whose holds on Legislature seats are tenuous."[161]

Some delegates claimed that the usual sources of party funds were already drying up because of the proposed scrutiny of contributions. They speculated on the reputedly huge war-chest available to the Union Nationale, an election fund which was probably far greater than the disposable fund of the Liberals.

However, since the leadership desired it, and since the committees recommended it, and most of the delegates were content to go along, although they expressed some reservations, a number of sweeping resolutions were adopted by the convention in plenary session.

RESOLUTIONS ADOPTED ON ELECTORAL REFORM

(1) the Convention recommended: the compulsory nomination of an election agent responsible for each candidate;

(2) that the State assume a number of specified expenses for all candidates;

(3) reimburse candidates proportionate to the number of voters on the list, to be paid to each candidate gaining a minimum of 20 per cent of the vote, plus an additional grant for candidates in constituencies of large areas;

(4) contribute for certain specified expenses of parties up to the amount of 10 cents per elector, these to be made only to a party which has a leader, a program, candidates in 50 per cent of the constituencies, and obtains a minimum of 10 per cent of the total vote;

(5) that expenditures of candidates be limited to 50 cents per elector and that of parties to 20 cents per elector;

(6) that costs of publicity should be limited to rates not to exceed so-called national rates;

(7) that each candidate and party should be compelled to publish a report of all electoral expenditures;

(8) that party expenses should be subsidized between elections, a rate of 5 cents per elector, annually;

(9) that the government study the possibility of controlling the origin of

candidates' and parties' campaign funds, including forbidding parties accepting contributions from persons or organisms not qualified as provincial electors;

(10) and finally that the *ELECTION ACT* be administered by a quasi-judicial commission of three permanent members presided over by a judge.

PUBLIC REACTIONS

Premier Lesage concluded that the approved resolutions would put Quebec in the forefront of democratic nations.[162] The proposals, he said, would be submitted to the Legislature at the next session. Press reaction to the work of the convention and to Premier Lesage's closing speech was generally favourable, except for the Union Nationale's *MONTREAL-MATIN*, which was naturally rather skeptical of the whole business. *THE MONTREAL STAR* was obviously impressed and wondered if perhaps the Liberals were not going a bit far for their own good.[163] In other papers the first reaction was to establish comparisons or, rather, differences between the conventions of the two major parties, less than two months apart. Many remarked on the seriousness of the Liberals as compared with the fanfare of the Union Nationale's leadership convention.

Few papers discussed the content of the resolutions adopted, preferring simply either to give or to summarize the text. Most papers seemed to begin to be convinced that, in dealing with a subject as sensitive as electoral reform, the Liberal party really meant what it said about basic changes in the political life of the province.

Skepticism, which was common before the convention, began to give way to a grudging belief in the validity of what they had witnessed. It was said that the reform wing was in control, and trickery like the Union Nationale's celebrated Bill 34.[164] would not be repeated now, with the Liberals in the saddle.

THE LEGISLATIVE DEBATE

The Throne Speech announced:

> You will be called upon to legislate on two matters of prime importance: the revision of the *ELECTION ACT* and ... This will involve legislation as difficult as it is indispensable, designed as it must be to ensure the proper functioning of democracy.[165]

Early in the session (February 7, 1962) Premier Lesage introduced the new *QUEBEC ELECTION ACT* (Bill 15). It was a 219-page document and he explained that it contained three basic reforms:
1. Limitations of expenses of political parties and candidates in election campaigns: Contribution by the provincial treasury to expenses of candidates;
3. Various changes in time limits concerning elections (which would also have the effect of reducing their costs).

ANALYSIS OF BILL 15

On first reading the Bill contained: limitations of electoral expenditures of candidates to 50 cents per elector, and those of parties to 25¢, the payment by the provincial treasury of a part of candidate expenses up to 15¢ per elector and up to 25¢ in the three largest constituencies (by area). These and other provisions were to be enforced by fines and imprisonment as well as the voiding of an election, the loss of the right to vote, and disqualification as a candidate for six years for candidates and party leaders.

"Recognised Political Parties " were defined as a party wishing to incur election expenses to appoint an official agent through its recognised leader, the DGE to be informed in writing. The party had at the previous election to have had candidates in at least 3/5 of the constituencies, or have such number at the present election. If it does not attain such number the appointment is cancelled and it shall cease to be a recognised party. This definition was extremely important, for only such a party would have the right to spend any money at all during an election campaign.

Each candidate was to nominate an official agent, and no nomination paper would be valid unless accompanied by such an appointment. No expenditure might be made without this agent's signature. Newspapers, radio and TV stations which accepted advertising from a candidate or party without such a signature might be prosecuted for corrupt practices. Candidates' official agents had to submit a return of election expenses to the Returning Officer on a prescribed form, accompanied by invoices, receipts and other vouchers, within 60 days after the declaration of the elected candidate. Similarly each party's official agent was to submit the party's return to the DGE within 120 days following that fixed for the return of the writs.

PUBLICITY REQUIREMENTS

The Returning Officer would publish, in a prescribed form, a summary of each candidate's return in local newspapers (in French and in English) within IO days of receipt, while the CEO (DGE) would publish summaries of party expenses in the *QUEBEC OFFICIAL GAZETTE* within 15 days of receipt. The returning officers would allow electors to examine the returns and other documents for the ensuing 180 days and then deliver them to the candidates on request or destroy them while the CEO (DGE) would allow electors to examine party returns and associated documents for the same time span and then return them to the recognised party leader on request or destroy them. Severe penalties were fixed for contraventions, specified to be corrupt practices.

FINANCIAL AID

The government would aid candidates financially in various ways. It would supply free 20 copies of electoral lists. It would pay poll representatives of the candidates of the two parties which had received the most votes in the last election. In addition, as briefly noted, the candidates of the two parties which had obtained the most votes in the last election, and any other candidate who obtained at least 20 per cent of the vote, he would have the right to receive 15 cents per elector — and for his election expenses.

What would be the total limitation and the total cost of these provisions? There would be about 2.8 million electors listed at the next election (which was 1962 and then 1966). Thus the total expenditures of each party would be limited to $700,000 for the general campaign. If the party ran candidates in all ridings, the total electoral expenditures of all its candidates combined might not exceed $1.4M. The total sum that a party and its candidates might expend would amount to a maximum of $2.lM According to this writer's calculations, the minimum extra cost to the provincial treasury for reimbursement, assuming that only two candidates ran per riding, would have been about $1,918,700. As we will see, in the Bill as enacted in 1963 the costs were considerably higher.

PUBLIC REACTIONS

The newspapers felt that the discussions in committee would be lively and controversial. It was immediately seen that the definition of the "recognised party" would be the most debated as the Union Nationale (and others) held that the necessity of running candidates in 60 per cent of the ridings was somewhat excessive. Premier Lesage said that this level was set by cabinet, because only such a group "would have a chance of forming a government." He added that the total expense limitation would be, from his knowledge of Quebec elections, much, much less than had been spent for decades.

He declared that his government would accept no back-sliding on its main principles, which he defined as the limitation of the expenditures of parties and candidates, and the participation by the government in the expenses of candidates. The government had the intention of going still further in its experiment of the state-financing of election expenses but he did not wish to compromise by going too far at once. He felt it was an honest attempt, which would certainly revolutionize concepts about elections, even on a national scale. (The federal government took the plunge with the federal Election Expenses Act in 1974).

In first reactions *THE MONTREAL STAR* called the bill "revolutionary." In an editorial entitled "An Election Act Looking to Reform" it felt that if the new Act left the Legislature in anything like its initial form, it should go far to curb the vicious election practices which had been all too readily accepted as normal in the past. In *LA PRESSE,* Vincent Prince was more skeptical but still favoured the bill. If law could force consciences and impose virtue," he wrote, "I should be tempted to proclaim that the Bill ... will finally rid us, once for all, of the immoral grip of election funds and of the dubious practices of which appeals to the people have been too often the opportunity here."

There came some dissenting voices: President Roger Provost of the QFL (Quebec Federation of Labour) and President Romeo Mathieu of the provincial New Democratic Party, said that the proposed electoral reform contained weaknesses that bordered on a conspiracy against democracy. It would do nothing to assure better labour representation in the Legislative Assembly and although it was "excellent" in principle that the State should limit election expenses and pay a part of them itself, they doubted if the proposed legislation would limit campaign spending effectively.

There was also some comment from Ontario, whose political leaders were divided. John Wintermeyer, then Liberal leader, said he would like to see a similar Bill in Ontario, while Donald MacDonald, NDP leader, criticised what he said was a threat to some basic political rights.

Within Quebec, the Opposition leader, Daniel Johnson, reacted with a well thought-out critique, calling the proposals a "dangerous, anti-democratic and retrograde move" unless drastically amended. He hoped the Legislature committee would be able to bring major amendments. As presented, it would discriminate against a third party by not allowing it to spend any money whatsoever on general party expenses. The proposed reforms would give the party in power a decided advantage, would remove safeguards, and would be unjust to "other" party candidates and Independents because they would not be identified on the ballot. He thought it was good to have smaller parties and Independents whether they are "nationalist, democratic, separatists or whatever." Such groups not only would be prevented from spending as parties but would have to find the money to pay their poll representatives. Mr. Johnson said the Union Nationale, which he claimed had no federal wing, was at a special disadvantage. "There's nothing to stop the federal Liberal party from putting out propaganda for the provincial party, " he said. He did agree that the idea of providing 15 cents per elector per candidate from the provincial treasury was "an experiment which should be tried" but he described as "visionary" attempts to control party spending when "no party is obliged to make public its election revenues."

Premier Lesage replied that the Bill was a start. "One day the State would absorb all election expenses," he declared "thus rendering party funds useless." He held to the definition of "recognised party" for a party, to be serious, must have a reasonable, or at least mathematical chance of forming a government." This principle did not harm the NDP for if it wanted to arrive in power it would have to have candidates in at least 60 per cent of the constituencies. The Premier said that it would be easy enough to control electoral expenditures for "in addition to the precautions provided by the law, candidates and party leaders will be strongly interested in evaluating their opponents' expenditures." He concluded that the Bill was not perfect, but it was an innovation in Canada, and a first step toward the disappearance of election funds, and the state payment of election expenditures.

Andre Laurendeau summarised the opening public debate in a *LE DEVOIR* editorial:[166]

There are already formulated harsh critiques about the Bill. Some are partisan, others pertinent. Moreover nothing is more normal than this examination, nothing is healthier. However, on the whole, this *ELECTION ACT* ... has an incontestable superiority over those which preceded it. In many ways it is courageous and audacious. The idea of limiting electoral expenditure is an innovation in Quebec. To reject it- -as a Union Nationale member did on television—because this would be to show the country that our elections are scandalously expensive, is a pitiful argument. The country knows perfectly well our practices and the size of our electoral funds. What it learns today is our Will to reform.

To make the state take part of the legitimate expenses of the parties corresponds to a just idea: it is a question of permitting the parties to escape, to a certain extent, from the tyranny of the fund contributors. It is right, equally, to recognize the existence of parties officially and no longer only those of the government and the official opposition. The attitude of the past becomes more hypocritical, it tended also to protect the old parties. It would be unjust to forget that this Bill represents important progress over past legislation, and a sincere effort to overcome the difficulties of our environment. I find in it also a sense of risk, for the legislator does not fear to go beyond the beaten path. Let us recognize first of all goodwill where we find it, and especially when we meet it where it has always been so rare.

COMMITTEE STUDY, DEBATE AND AMENDMENTS

In clause-by-clause study, Paul Gerin-Lajoie declared for the government that election expenses in Quebec had constituted a scandal, an orgy in the eyes of the people of Quebec and of the rest of Canada. Limitation of expenses was one of the principles from which the government would not budge. Considering that the government would meet some expenses the total allowed was more than ample. He declared that among the other principles from which the government would not budge were the legal recognition of parties and government financial aid to candidates.

Mr. Johnson said his party hoped to make the final Act more democratic and less retrograde than that proposed. The Union Nationale would attempt not only to obtain amendments to details but to sections covering what it considered principles.

Mr. Gerin-Lajoie said that as a means of controlling election expenses, the government specified the restrictions on official agents, making them legally responsible for expenses and providing severe penalties for infractions of the law. He said that since the government would pay some expenses, this would go a long way toward limiting the dangers of party war-chests. In answering criticisms, Youth Minister Gerin-Lajoie insisted that, in granting political parties an official status, the law did not foresee only the two main parties now operating. He said, in a notable admission, that the 60 per cent rule was a matter of detail, and that the exact percentage could be a matter for the Committee.

A week later, after hearing a brief by the QFL (Quebec Federation of Labour) Premier Lesage suggested an amendment that would ease restrictions on third parties. If such a party decided to run candidates in, for instance, 20 ridings, it might be worth giving it the right to spend 25 cents per elector in those ridings. (As we will see, he went still further on final enactment, giving such rights to a party running only 10). He had obviously felt the criticism, for he insisted that he wanted to overcome the impression that the government was trying to protect the two major parties and wanted to restrain third parties.

Later, in the Assembly, the principle of a flat-rate limitation on expenditure was raised and its replacement by a sliding scale was advocated by Paul Dozois (UN-Montreal-St. James) and later adopted. The effect of the scale adopted was to reduce the limitation, rather than raising it, which was apparently Mr. Dozois' original intention. The one he put forward for debate would have set a limit of 75 cents per elector for the first 10,000 electors, 60 cents for the next 10,000 and 50 cents for every elector over 20,000. The section was suspended for further consideration.

Union Nationale members also had some hard thoughts about the official agent requirement. By simply spending more than the law permits, the agent could get the candidate banned from holding office. Mr. Gerin-Lajoie remarked that such candidates could act as their own official agents.

The same day the government answered its critics with a drastic change as to what should constitute an official party. A party must have 10 candidates to be "recognised. " The 10-candidate requirement would hold throughout the Act.

On June 10 the Committee accepted the principle of a sliding scale of expenditures for candidates that would permit those in small ridings to spend relatively more and those in larger ones, less. Mr. Dozois' suggestion was thus accepted, but modified to 60, 50 and 40 cents. This concluded the Committee's work.

On July 6, Bill 15, *THE QUEBEC ELECTIONS ACT*, as amended, was agreed to and was read the third time on division.[167] (The government planned to introduce it in the Legislative Council — upper house — in November. But on September 22 it dissolved the Legislature and called an election for November 14, 1962. This, of course, meant that Bill 15 died on the Order Paper. It would have no bearing on the 1962 election, and would have to be revived, if so desired, by the next government).

BILL 15 AS ADOPTED IN 1962

The Bill, as given third reading on July 6, was essentially the same as that given first reading five months before, except for the two major amendments described. Candidates were now to be allowed to spend up to 60 cents per elector for the first 10,000, 50 cents per elector for the second 10,000 and 40 cents in excess of 20,000 — in general elections; in by-elections these could be increased by 25 cents per elector. In the three largest-area ridings, the maxima were increased by 10 cents per elector.

The new definition of "recognised party"' now meant a party with at least 10 candidates either at the last or present election. Only such a party could appoint an official agent and spend any money in its general campaign.

ENACTMENT

Since the Liberal party easily won the 1962 election, there was no problem to reintroducing Bill 15, if the will were there. It was, and during the 1963 session Bill 15 was reintroduced and went from first reading to sanction without substantial amendment to the provisions on political financing. The only substantial change was Section 219 (Frank Hanley's amendment) to give an elected Independent member all the privileges in the Act given to a party MLA. Also the salary of the CEO (now DGE —Directeur general des elections — was raised to $18,000 per annum.

REMARKS

In a sense these party-financing provisions are self-enforcing. The limitation for candidate spending is tied to the maximum reimbursement. If a candidate overspends, not only is it an offence, but he cannot be reimbursed for the "extra" spending. In addition, every candidate who might be reimbursed, cannot be unless/until his report is received. This makes for maximum compliance. However, the guarantee of reimbursement for nearly all candidates of the two major parties, was remarked upon negatively then, and is still remarked on — as a giant fraud — even now.[168]

In the first session after the 1962 election Mr. Johnson (Opposition Leader) began the debate on the reintroduced Bill 15 by claiming that the Liberals had not wanted the new Election Act for the 1962 election since they would have been beaten. Had they been serious in claims to purity, he said, it could have been passed in an hour by the Legislative Council. He went further and said that even if the old Act had been decently enforced the Liberals would now be in the opposition. He added, "The population had watched in stupor the election tactics used by the Liberals."

The only substantial amendment was one that would profoundly alter the operation. It came, unanimously, on March 7. It reduced the voting age to 18 from 21, and so would enfranchise well over a quarter-million new voters. At one stroke this would enable each party with candidates in all ridings to spend over $62,000 more on its general campaign and its candidates to spend upward of $125,000 more.

This time the Bill was submitted to the Legislative Council and the fears of a year before regarding the Union Nationale's possible last-ditch opposition or amendments of substance in the Upper House were not realised. On July 10, 1963 the Bill was given Royal Assent as the *QUEBEC ELECTION ACT*, 1963, chapter 13, and in the following year it became part of the *REVISED STATUTES OF QUEBEC* as the *ELECTION ACT*, 1964, chapter 7.

Four by-elections (in 1964) saw the advent of a unique experiment in North America, the partial payment of campaign expenses by a government.

APPLICATION

The following general election took place on June 5, 1966. In the four by-elections under the Act we can conclude that the financial clauses of the new Act worked well in their first test. The limits were set by the Returning Officers and were apparently respected. The returns were made in good form and were duly published in local newspapers and, finally, the government paid up (and all its candidates were elected). The stage was set for the general election but not before the government reviewed its experience and decided that some far-reaching amendments were in order. These were made in the 1965 session.

FURTHER AMENDMENTS: BILL 49 OF 1965

The government's direction in party financing became clearer when the expenses for maintaining a recognised party's permanent office in Montreal and Quebec City were included. This, we will see, is one step in an ever-increasing subsidization of Quebec parties by their government. After reviewing its experience with the "little general election" of October 5, 1964, the government decided that the new Election Act required further tinkering. Apart from the party offices, the most important change was a substantial increase in reimbursement to candidates, but the opportunity was also taken to add to the items that need not be considered as election expenses and so would not be considered for reimbursement. These included the candidates' $200 deposit.[169]

On May 1, 1965 Premier Lesage announced consideration of raising the reimbursement rate for candidates from 15 cents to 30 cents per elector. He declared that the "democratic ideal" was to make elections as reasonable as possible by making people more conscious of civic duties and so to reduce campaign expenses, such as publicity, circulars, etc. Apparently the original draft intended to pay all the expenses of candidates above 20 cents per elector so as to leave only 5 cents of permissible expenses. The effect of the amendment is to approximately double the amount of reimbursement to most candidates if they are candidates of the two major parties or those who obtain at least 20 per cent of the votes. This was brought out by Municipal Affairs Minister Pierre Laporte in Committee of the Whole on July 13.

He said:

1. At present candidates can only spend a certain amount of money per elector ... The ceiling varies from 40 to 60 cents a voter, depending on population. For most candidates the ceiling is 50 cents. At present, the government pays back 15 cents a voter to any candidate who gets 20 per cent or more of the ballots cast. [170]

2. In a riding where the number of electors is between 10,000 and 20,000— the majority of ridings — the maximum is 50 cents (per elector) a candidate. Under the amendment, a candidate would receive the usual 15 cents per voter plus one-fifth of expenses per elector between 15 and 40 cents, plus everything he pays out over 40 cents. This would mean a candidate paying the full 50 cents would pay 20 cents out of his own pocket and the government would hand him back 30 cents.

3. In a riding where the population is less than 10,000 the ceiling is 60 cents an elector. Here the government would pay the candidate the usual, 15 cents plus one-fifth of what he spends between this amount and 40 cents plus anything he spends over 40 cents. This means he would receive 40 cents per voter from the government and would have to pay 20 cents out of his own pocket.

In the debate, Premier Lesage cited the measure as an example of government plans to eliminate the system of political slush funds by limiting expenses and helping candidates who get 20 per cent or more of the ballots. By August 6, 1965, Bill 49 had passed the Legislative Council and was given Royal Assent as 13-14 Eliz II, 1965, c. 12 & 13.

We will now summarize the political finance provisions of the Election Act.

POLITICAL FINANCE PROVISIONS

Apart from the new reporting requirements, the new sections are those dealing with expenditures NOT to be considered as election expenses (s. 372); new reimbursement scales (s.380); and the filing and retention of documents provision already mentioned (s.382). Incidentally, the DGE was also given a further raise from $18,000 to $22,500 per annum (s.8).

LIMITATIONS

Parties were still limited to no more than 25 cents per elector, in the total of ridings in which they have candidates in general elections: no general campaign expenditures allowed for by-elections. Candidates were allowed to spend up to 60 cents per elector for the first 10,000, 50 cents per elector for the second 10,000 and 40 cents per elector in excess of 20,000, all during general elections. In four special ridings (three large area and the Islands of Iles de la Madeleine) the maxima were increased by 10 cents per elector. "Recognised party" means the Premier's party or that of the leader of the Official Opposition and a party with at least 10 official candidates in the last election or in the election in progress. Only such a party may appoint an official agent and spend any money on its general campaign.

REIMBURSEMENT

There is no reimbursement for party campaigns (the route taken as we will see, is to subsidize them outside the election period). Candidates were to be reimbursed by the DGE up to 15 cents per listed elector for election expenses as specified and shown as paid; that is, candidates who are declared elected, or who have obtained at least 20 per cent of the valid vote, or who are entitled to paid poll representatives under Section 219 (these are the candidates of the two major parties). In addition, the DGE will pay an amount equal to one-fifth of election expenses in excess of 15 cents, but not in excess of 40 cents per elector, and all election expenses in excess of 40 cents per elector. He will not, however, pay the *additional* 25 cents per elector allowed to candidates in by-elections. Naturally the previous section — to reimburse candidates up to 25 cents per elector in the three large-area constituencies — is struck out.

OTHER ASSISTANCE

Returning Officers to send 20 copies of voters- lists to each nominated candidate. Poll representatives (candidates' agents) to be paid at the same rate as a poll clerk ($32) for election day. These to be nominated by candidates declared elected at the last election (applies also to sitting Independents) or by candidates of recognised parties (highest or second highest in voting)

AGENCY

Every candidate and every recognised party must appoint an official agent. No nomination is valid unless accompanied by the appointment of the candidate's official agent, and a party wishing to incur election expenses must have its "recognised leader" (not defined) appoint an official agent. Such an agent who exceeds the permissible expenditures, or files a false return is guilty of a corrupt practice, and thus liable to a fine of from .$100-$1,000 and to imprisonment from one to twelve months and his political rights revoked for six years. During an election no person other than the official agent of a candidate or of a recognised party may incur election expenses.

ELECTION EXPENSES

These are given a wide definition and mean all the expenditures incurred in an election (*EXCEPT* those specified in s.372.2) to promote or oppose the election of a candidate or party, or to approve or disapprove the steps recommended or opposed by them. NOT included is the necessary cost of a nomination convention, including the expenses of the candidate chosen, the cost of renting halls and the convening of delegates, but it may not include any publicity and may not exceed the sum of $1,000 (new amount). All payments for election expenses of $10 or more must be proved by an itemized invoice.

RETURNS AND PUBLICITY

This paragraph is all new. Each official agent must deliver a return of expenses to the Returning Officer, who must publish a summary of it in both French and English newspapers. The Returning Officer keeps all documents and makes them available and then sends them to the CEO, who keeps them for a year and then returns them to the candidate or destroys them. Similar provisions apply to parties. In the case of returns not being made the candidate or party leader would be disqualified from sitting in the Legislature until they have been.

ENFORCEMENT

The quasi-judicial commission which was suggested to enforce the Act, never put in an appearance. So far the CEO (DGE) has been in full charge. *NOMENCLATURE*: At the time of enactment of Bill 15, the chief electoral officer was termed the Chief Returning Officer or in French le President-general des elections. I have used the more generic terms of CEO Chief Electoral Officer and the more recent DGE Directeur general des elections.

As the Parti Quebecois took over in 1976 there was an upheaval and soon there were three Directors-general: one for the Financing of Political Parties; a second for Electoral Representation; and yet a third as a catch-all Directeur general des elections. Of course, this system was very expensive and, during the recession of 1981-83, the two "extra" directors general were abolished and since then the DGE has been in full charge. But since Bill 15 the DGE who supervises the carrying-out of the Act is appointed by the Legislature acting by resolution. He is given the status and tenure of a district judge. He is ordered to".... devote his time exclusively to the performance of his duties."

The CEO testified before a Legislature committee that the cost of elections in this province would triple as a result of the political finance provisions of the new *ELECTION ACT*. He said that the cost to the provincial treasury will increase to between \$8 million and \$10 million from about \$3 millions.[171]

THE 1966 ELECTION (June 5): FINANCES

This election was the first for Bill 15 to receive a full test. This writer made an examination of its operation. Since the writing and publication of this study (in its original form) could not be delayed, my unofficial estimates were employed. But final figures have been interpolated.

This section covers the operation of the financial provisions of the *QUEBEC ELECTION ACT* in its first large-scale test in the 1966 election. These provisions may be subsumed under two general headings: (1) maxima imposed on expenditures, covering parties and candidates; (2) reimbursements of election expenses, which are granted to candidates only. A final section deals with impressions of the campaign.

MAXIMA ON EXPENDITURES

Recognised Parties

There were four "recognised" parties: the Liberal party of the Premier; the Union Nationale (UN) of the Leader of the official opposition (each of which had a full slate of 108 candidates);and the Ralliement National (RN) with 80 candidates; and the Rassemblement pour l'Indépendance Nationale (RIN) with 73. Three other parties had candidates: the Parti Socialiste de Québec (PSQ) the Quebec Conservative Party (QCP); and the Communist Party with four candidates each. None of these qualified as "recognised" and therefore they were not permitted to spend money on any general campaign. While the names of the recognised parties appeared on the ballots for the first time, the names of the unrecognised parties did not. Also in the running were 27 assorted Independents.

Election expenses for a party during elections had to be limited so as not to exceed 25 cents per elector in the total of ridings in which such party has candidates. Table 1 shows the maximum permissible expenditures on the general campaign for each of the four recognised parties. A later addition is the last column which shows the later declared expenditures of the four parties.

CANDIDATES' MAXIMA

We have seen that the election expenses for each candidate had never to exceed 60 cents per elector up to 10,000, and in general elections 50 cents per elector up to 20,000, and 40 cents over that number (20,000). In the ridings of Abitibi-East, Iles de la Madeleine, Duplessis and Saguenay, the maximum is increased by 10 cents.

In the original study for the Committee on Election Expenses there was included a Table 6 which showed all candidates' maximum permissible expenditure in all ridings.[172] It showed that the maximum permissible spending for the 418 candidates ranged from the lowest — $4,627.70 — in Iles de la Madeleine to the highest of $30,366.80 in Terrebonne. The total amount which might have been spent in any riding was a function of the maximum per candidate multiplied by the

TABLE I

LEGAL MAXIMA OF PARTY EXPENDITURES ON GENERAL CAMPAIGN, & DECLARED EXPENDITURES—1966

PARTY	TOTAL CANDIDATES	TOTAL OF LISTED ELECTORS	MAXIMUM PERMISSABLE EXPENDITURE	DECLARED EXPENDITURE[72]
		$	$	
Liberal	108	3,190,373	797,593.25	688,287.56
U.N.	108	3,190,373	797,593.25	588,666.46
R.N.	90	2,786,559	696,639.75	15,513.24
R.I.N.	73	2,508,705	627,176.25	17,108.07
Total maximum permissible expenditures by all recognized parties:			2,919,002.50	1,309,575.35

Sources: For column 5 of Table I: *Quebec Official Gazette*, V. 98, No. 40, Oct. 8, 1966; Vol. 98, No. 45, p.5825, Nov. 12, 1966; V.98, p.5923, Nov. 19, 1966; V.99, No. 2, p. 170, Jan. 14, 1967; No. 51, p. 6525, Dec. 24, 1966.

number of candidates. Thus the maximum which might have been spent
in a riding ranged from the three lowest $9,255.40 in Iles de la
Madeleine, $10,170. 80 in Huntingdon and $10,857.60 in Yamaska,
each of which had only two candidates, to the three highest of
$138,556.80 in Robert Baldwin, $133,720.80 in Laval and $128,630.40
in Westmount. The large populations of ridings on Montreal Island were
reflected in the fact that while the average maximum per candidate for
the whole province was $14, 728.30, the average for Montreal Island was
$20,021.76. A large number of candidates also ran in Montreal ridings.
Thus the average maximum permitted expenditure for Montreal ridings
was $95,831. 80 compared to $60,074.40 per riding in the province as a
whole. In general, the ridings in which most might have been spent were
not those in which a great deal*was* actually spent. These are the Montreal
ridings with traditionally fringe parties' candidates. Having run their
candidates these groups seem to think that is all that is required. They
spend, usually, only nominal amounts. And since these ridings have
large populations, the regular party candidates have leeway for their
spending.

Over the whole province the total possible legal expenditures by
candidates was $6,488,036.20. But it is not suggested that anything like
this amount was actually spent.

REIMBURSEMENT

All official Liberals and all official Union Nationale candidates,
except the one in Ste-Anne, as well as Mr. Frank Hanley, the Independent
member for that seat, were guaranteed reimbursement regardless of how
few votes they might poll. The Union Nationale candidates who
qualified for reimbursement include 15 who lost their deposits. Only
nine candidates qualified under the "20 per cent of the vote" rule. The
other six qualified under the Section 219 rule (even in Duplessis, where
the Union Nationale won only about two per cent of the vote). Some of
these received far fewer votes than other candidates who did not qualify
for reimbursement. In fact none of the other candidates who lost their
deposits achieved 20 per cent of the vote, although several came close,
and none is therefore qualified.

It appeared that 226 candidates qualified for a total of $1,992,383.50,
or an average of $8,815.86 per candidate. Among these are the full slates
of the Liberal and 107 Union Nationale candidates, each slate qualifying

for a total of $952,544.70, four candidates for $32,881.10, a single RIN candidate (its leader, Pierre Bourgault, in Duplessis riding) for $8,429.20 and five Independents for a total possible of $46,001.80.

OTHER ASSISTANCE

(a) *Voters' lists*. For the first time in a Quebec election 20 copies of the voters' lists in each poll were supplied to each candidate. No firm estimate could be made of this expense to the treasury, but an average of $1,500 per candidate may be realistic in view of remarks made at the time this provision was under debate in the Legislature. With 418 candidates the charge could be of the order of $627,000.

(b) *Payment of roll Representatives*: Also for the first time in a Quebec election the provision that two candidates in each riding might appoint an agent in each poll, to be paid the same as a Poll Clerk ($30 plus $2 for meals). In this election a total of 16,531 polls were established. Two agents in each poll at $32 amounts to a total charge of $1,057,984.

IMPRESSIONS OF THE CAMPAIGN AND OF THE ACT

Francois Drouin, Quebec's President-général of Elections, estimated the new cost to the treasury of elections under Bill 15, as triple that before (from about $3 millions to between $8 and $10 millions). It appeared later that this was an over-estimate. Perhaps a "little more than double" would be more correct. This writer's estimate was that the new cash cost to the treasury in 1966 would be something over $3.5 millions.

On the whole the 1966 campaign does not seem to have been characterized by large spending by parties and candidates. A comment made by an editorial in *THE MONTREAL STAR* sums up its financial aspect most succinctly:[173]

> If the provincial election seems quiet, almost lack-lustre, political style, lack of issues is certainly not the reason. There is plenty of both. What has dulled the colour and dampened the fireworks is the new election act which is having its first large-scale try-out and showing every sign of working effectively.

The good old days of wild and reckless spending have gone, at least in most areas ...

The Act is not perfect. Certain of its provisions seem on the basis of experience so far to be unnecessarily limiting. But for the most part it appears to be doing a good job of reducing the kind of excesses with which we were familiar not so long ago.

The considered opinion of Claude Ryan, Editor/Publisher of *LE DEVOIR*, four months after the election, was that:

Whatever the result, the last election in Quebec was an honest one ... Secret election funds of the past were not entirely absent, but occult financing was not a major factor in deciding the outcome of the election. (174)

Vincent Lemieux of Laval University and Louis Massicotte of Ottawa's Parliamentary library have pointed out certain flaws in the Act, particularly the inequitability of the provision which requires candidates of third parties to obtain at least 20 per cent of the votes to qualify for reimbursement, while the candidates of the two major parties are not thus restricted.[175]

But on the whole, both concluded that this is an excellent law. "In the last election the Act eliminated a good part if not the whole of the advantage which the government-party used to have over the opposition because of a generally better provided campaign fund."

In other words, the *ELECTION ACT* did the job that was set for it. At a stroke, it transformed Quebec's elections, always reputedly among the most expensive in Canadian provincial politics, into among the least expensive. To some extent, the expense was transferred from the parties and their candidates to the public treasury. But, as we saw, the previous party expense, in the case of a government-party, came largely from the treasury anyway, in the corrupt form of kickbacks and other now-illegal methods.

CHAPTER FOUR: BOURASSA'S SUBSIDY OF 1975 AND LEVESQUE'S SUBSIDY OF 1977

The first Quebec measure specifically on party financing was the ELECTION ACT of 1963. Of course, Quebec's parties were financed before 1963, as well as after. The point is that these finances might be assisted by the public treasury and this era commenced fully in Quebec in 1963, as for Canada as a whole.

Most party financing systems in Canada favor the method of reimbursement of specific expenditures. Quebec governments have also taken a different route, that of subsidizing the parties' funds directly and leaving it up to them to use this "extra" cash how they choose.

As we have seen in the previous chapter, the policy began with Bill 15. In its financing provisions there were limits put on the spending of parties and candidates. Some candidates were privileged to receive reimbursement of part of their expenditure. But in the same Act, there was a little-publicised provision for the treasury to pay the expenses of a permanent party office in Montreal and Quebec City.

Already, this measure favoured the two major parties. Virtually all of their candidates would be reimbursed and their office expenses would be paid. Third parties do not maintain "permanent"offices unless they become (like the Union Nationale in its time, and the Parti Québécois in the 1970s) a major party.

Bill 15 limited election spending and justified this by reimbursing many candidates. Where was there to go now? The parties wanted new, easy money and Premier Robert Bourassa gave it to them — a straight subsidy of $400,000 total, to be divided between the major parties on the basis of their votes at the previous election.

So, what we can call the subsidy route began in 1965 (payment of office expenses —incidentally just one year after the organizational split between the Quebec Liberal Party and the National Liberal Federation (Quebec) with the partial easing through payment of office expenses.

Then, in 1975, Premier Bourassa's Liberal government went further and gave parties, with seats in the Assembly, a direct subsidy, the first in Canada. But we may note that in Europe this is the usual method — to give cash subsidies for the parties to spend as they choose.

Bourassa's subsidy did not last long, nor did Bourassa's government after 1975. The rest of this book is more or less about Bill 2: *An Act to Govern the Financing of Political Parties.* [193] This legislation was considered so important by the Levesque (Parti Québécois—PQ) government that it was the second bill they tabled (after Bill 1 [101] in 1977). Most of Bill 2 deals with the sources of party financing. But, often overlooked, is a perhaps more important section — the party subsidy.

The plan for this is that the Levesque government took the Bourassa subsidy and raised its amount, quite considerably. In the official terms: The relative portion of the treasury in the financing of parties was increased. The annual allocation was set at 25 cents per name on the electoral list.

There is currently nearly five million dollars annually to be distributed to the parties. However, a party had to have at least 12 seats in the Assembly, or 20 percent of the provincial vote. Thus, the Equality Party, with only four members after 1989, did not qualify.

Actually, now the provision "with seats in the Assembly" has been changed. In 1994, 12 Quebec political parties received a government subsidy, based on their vote at the last election. The total amount granted was $4,960,043. But the two major parties got the lion's share--together 91.4 prcent of the total. The QLP received $2,300,204 and the PQ $2,231,088. The next largest amount was for the Equality Party-- $177,566, followed a long way behind by the NDP with $78,354, and ADQ with $71,087 and the Natural Law Party with $52,141, and the Green Party received $36, 271, the Lemon Party got $9,750 and no other party was in the thousands, although Sovereignty-Quebec received $1,618 and the Communist Party had $1,085.

CONCLUSION: CHAPTER FOUR:

The conclusion is that in a fairly short period (ten or eleven years) the two major Quebec provincial parties have been able to replace much of the money they once had to scramble for (in the slush fund, bagman technique) with "clean" money, regularly received from the public treasury. The effects have been drastic, on the political system, on the structure of the party system and, not least, on the internal organization of the parties themselves.

Of course, Bill 2 is much more than this, which is why we spend the rest of this book to deal with it and its effects.

CHAPTER FIVE: BILL 2 OF 1977

Even for the political leaders who used them and lived by them, "occult funds" (in English "secret" or "slush", the usual term in French is "occult") were anathema, at least in public utterance.

We saw Jean Lesage earlier, during debate on Bill 15, citing this first great reform as an example of government plans to eliminate the system of political slush funds. Claude Ryan wrote "secret election funds" of the past were not entirely absent (from the 1966 election) but occult financing was not a major factor (indicating that this was a good thing).

But the Québec leader who was most outspoken against slush funds was Réné Levesque. As a rookie minister (of Hydraulic Resources in 1960) he had a short course in how powerful they can be. As Levesque put it later, of the "slush fund tradition: They (a Boston engineering firm) had a list of firms that contributed to the party. One firm had bridges in Montreal, another had roads — and this Boston firm had power plants."

"Do you know how long it took me to fight that (letter of intent) through?" Two months. As soon as I brought it up in Cabinet, I got a call from the senior lawyer of the Liberal party, the chief of fund-raising — who was also a corporate counsel for this god-damn Boston firm."

The reform that Levesque cherished the most was the party financing legislation, Bill 2.[177] Indeed, he expressed more emotion about political fund-raising than about anything else. His face would screw up with contempt and his vocabulary would suggest the swamp: "slime", "ooze", "shadowy".

What he called "the old slush-fund tradition" was part of Québec's political folklore; donations were secret, and were quietly repaid with government contracts. This was one of the reasons for the Liberal government's unsavory reputation: a crime probe witness saying in 1973 that underworld figures had contributed to Bourassa's leadership campaign, and Bourassa lamely conceding the possibility; police investigations of a Liberal MNA for election act violations in 1973; police leaks during the 1976 campaign alleging extortion from lottery distributors.

When Levesque gave Robert Burns the mandate to draw up the party-financing law, he knew it would be tough. Burns had constantly harassed the Bourassa government on the question, and had held up the Parti Québécois funding approach as a model. Partly from conviction, partly by necessity, the PQ raised money by going from door to door and made the donors' names public. In fact, fund-raising was a major part of the party's organizational activity. Burns set out to make party practice into law, and produced the first piece of legislation in the session — Bill 2, and its ban on corporate donations, was the first such law in the Western world.

The result of visits to Washington, Sacramento, Toronto and Ottawa was a sweeping bill based on a simple principle. Only voters would be allowed to contribute to political parties. Corporations, companies, clubs, associations, unions, cooperatives would no longer be allowed to make contributions. This was opposed by the Chambre de Commerce, the Liberals and, more importantly, by the Human Rights Commission, as restricting freedom of opinion, expression and association and they objected to the powers of search and seizure that were given to the new body, the office of the *Directeur general du financement des partis politiques*.

Burns announced that the search and seizure provision would be changed. But he would not budge on the fundamental question, saying that the government was determined to abolish secret election funds, "and no recommendation, no matter where it comes from, will make it back off on the subject."

The law reflected the PQ's belief that corporate donations were a crucial, occult factor in Québec politics. Bill 2 was intended to sever the link between corporate wealth and political parties. The Péquistes never thought that the Liberals would be capable of raising money from door to door; in fact, they did learn to do so. The result was to transform the nature of partisan politics in Québec.

The Parti Québécois' (PQ) Bill 2 deals mainly with contributions to parties and candidates. As Massicotte puts it: There is nothing astonishing about the fact that the PQ made the abolition of secret election funds its *priority* in electoral reform.[178]

Actually, the term "abolition" is excessive, as only contributions of over $100 need to be reported, and anonymous donations are allowed.[179] But all contributions from "moral persons — personnes morales" — corporations, unions and any association — are banned. In fact, the only kind of donor allowed is a Québec elector, up to an aggregate limit of $3,000 per party per year.[180]

TAX BREAKS

For the first time in Québec provincial party financing, tax breaks were allowed for political contributions. This feature greatly stimulated the rate of giving, as it had for federal parties after 1974 .

Finally, a control mechanism was established over the party financing regime. At first this was a *Director General of Political Party Financing*, separate from the DGE, but by 1983 this function was taken over by the present DGE.

By banning corporate contributions Bill 2 makes an effort to eliminate cadre parties, which rely on them. What has seemed to be left as a possibility for party financing is the (by now) classic "mass" party, depending on many small contributions. Réné Levesque chose this alternative for his new Parti Québécois, for a number of possible reasons.

MASS ("POPULAR") FINANCING — EFFECTIVENESS

The effectiveness of the mass party financing method is demonstrated by the fact that the Parti Québécois came to power only eight years after its foundation. In these eight years the party regulations specified that it would not take any large donations, and none from any "moral person." Of course, as a result, the PQ was always chronically short of funds; and we know *how* short, compared to the Liberals, at election time, from its reports on its election spending in 1970, 1973 and 1976.

While the Liberal party never failed to spend over 90 percent of its permitted (legal) maximum in these campaigns, whether it was the government or the opposition, the Parti Québécois spent only 31.3 percent in 1970, 44.3 percent in 1973 and, in 1976, when this party won the election, they spent only 76.8 per cent, compared to the Liberals' 97.7 per cent.[181]

IMMEDIATE EFFECTS

The apparent and rather immediate effect of Bill 2's complete ban on contributions from corporations, if effectively enforced, would be to destroy all previous fund-raising methods by all Québec provincial parties, except the Parti Québécois itself. But it is apparent that the Québec Liberal Party had considerable reserves for, in the 1981 election, although the PQ spent over 90 percent (97.2 per cent) of its permitted expenditures for the first (and so far only) time, still the QLP out-spent it, in defeat, with 98.5 percent.[182]

CENTRALIZATION & BUREAUCRATIZATION OF PARTIES

Since Bill 2 in 1977, there has been a rather great centralization and bureaucratization of Québec's parties. Massicotte comments: "An unwanted consequence is that a fundamentally voluntary activity is perhaps to pass into the hands of professionals who have the time to fill out the innumerable forms. The elitist character of political activity will be thus accentuated. A law has possibly accentuated the internal centralization of the parties. The authors have taken away the relatively decentralized nature of the Québec parties. Bill 2 has reduced the relative autonomy of their local and regional elements by subjecting their authorization, the appointment and firing of their official representatives, all to the pleasure of the party leaders. In pure law, a party leader may threaten a local or regional element with having its authorization withdrawn without having to indicate the least motive. The party element would thus lose the right to solicit and to collect contributions and to make expenditures, and the amounts in its possession could be seized by the State".[183]

DESTRUCTION OF MINOR PARTIES-QUÉBEC'S TWO-PARTY ELECTORAL LAW

Since 1977 there has been a rather great creation, and also destruction, of minor parties. We could define a "minor" party as one which has never elected a member of the House. Massicotte calls these small (minor) parties "the worst victims" of Bill 2. "By putting political financing into a myriad of detailed rules, the law has made their birth and their survival more of a problem, given the scope of the necessary resources, which they lack."[184]

The professionalization of political activity demands, especially, a complex machinery of permanent staff with an appropriate education, and the lack of such machinery increases the risk of errors, infractions and prosecutions ... Certainly the disappearance or break-up of third parties between 1976 and 1981 is chiefly due to the polarization around the (first) referendum, but it is legitimate to ask whether the new financial regime did not play a part. The distance between the old, well-established parties and the new movements was accentuated by the impossibility for the latter to benefit from public financing (since they had not elected a single member). Furthermore, by continuing to require from their candidates that they get at least 20 percent of the votes for reimbursement, while guaranteeing this advantage to the major party candidates, for their past performances, Bill 2 consolidated the fundamentally two-party character of Québec s electoral law.[185]

FUND-RAISING UNDER BILL 2

It is not necessary to analyze the complete table of the two major parties' fund-raising in the twelve years since Bill 2 to comprehend certain main trends. The Parti Québécois clearly had the advantage until 1983, with its two biggest years 1980 and 1981 (over and close to $4 millions each year). But, since 1984, when the Québec Liberal Party raised double the PQ, the QLP has broken the PQ's fund-raising records, and raised over $6 millions each year of 1985-6-7 and, in 1988, went through the roof with over $9 millions. In this period the PQ languished in the fund-raising doldrums.

The result of this PQ fund-raising drought was its inability to spend nearly as much as it was legally allowed in the two elections of 1985 and 1989, and the QLP's feast meant it could spend up to its limit.

Table II shows this situation in percentages: (It turned around in 1994:)

Table II

**Percentage of Maximum Expended in Elections
(1994 includes party campaigns plus candidates).**

	PQ	**QLP**
1985	72.2%	99.0%
1989	56.8%	99.4%
1994	92.2%	94.4%

The PQ's 1985 percentage of 72.2 is even lower than its percentage in 1976 — 76.8 — when it was on the way up. Its expenditure rate in 1989 was pitiful — a smaller proportion than the Union Nationale in the 1973 election (67.7%) when it was a third party, and in fact was shut out of the Assembly. If the PQ was to be a stable party, like any major party, then it must have a stable source of financing. It was apparent that "popular" financing, as the mass party method is usually called in Québec, as practised by the PQ over the years since its foundation in 1968, was not that source. But the alternative source seems to be "social activities", as practised by the QLP. Would the PQ turn to that source? In 1993-94 it did after it had said it never would.

It is possible that the latest PQ leader, Jacques Parizeau, once he had attained his first goal in the fund-raising area, of 100,000 party members, could organize them to improve his party's fund raising. But the PQ's best, at its peak, of $4 millions in each of 1980 and 1981 — was achieved with many more members — and so many more militants available. In any case, it still fails to match the QLP's totals over the past years.

Such fund-raising statistics may provide a new indicator to a premier about to call an election, if they have not already. After four poor fund-raising years, such as the PQ experienced before 1989, while the QLP's coffers were overflowing, Premier Bourassa must have felt quite safe, on this score, in calling the September 25, 1989 election.

How is it that under Bill 2's regime the PQ suffered while the QLP prospered? It is possible that the Péquiste militants, as well as the sympathizers who were contributors, were disheartened by the 1985 defeat and had not recovered from it.

Analysis of the vote in that election shows that most of the PQ vote loss may have been due to the abstentions by previous PQ voters. This feature, together with the known tens of thousands of Péquistes who dropped out of the party, mean that the fund-raising machine may have run down, as shown by its poor results as well as the stress put on this area by Parizeau as incoming leader. In any case, the internal dissensions and splits did not cease — perhaps they have now with Parizeau's accession. His first priority — to win, or win back — 100,000 members — shows that he gives fund raising a large place.

THE PROBLEM OF THE *MASS* PARTY

The difficulty for a mass party in raising funds during a period of its unpopularity I would call *the* problem of the mass party.[186] If we studied the phenomenon over a long period (say 50 years) we would see that there is a wave phenomenon — that while there are downs, which students grasp very well, there are also ups. So, although the PQ may never recapture its excitement of the years before 1984, it may become a more stable party, even if it cannot hope to scale the fund-raising summits of the QLP consistently, that is unless it copies some of its methods.

Successful door-to-door solicitation of funds in Québec does not seem possible with fewer than 100,000 members in a party, and it involves sending out an army of 15-20,000 militants to actually solicit; and this army must have reserves, and it must be organised and supplied. This is a considerable project, especially if it is conducted annually. It uses up infinitely more resources — in personnel, organization and money — than the cadre party's few bagmen collecting a few large cheques.

In terms of organization we find that the cadre party is much more efficient than the mass one. Its organization chart is a dream, but he who pays the piper calls the tune.

On the other hand, the QLP seems to have put the door-to-door technique aside. On a scale of 1-3, its Director General[187] placed it third for raising funds. He placed second the technique of going through membership lists to see who was "due" for another contribution; and first of all he put "social activities" — fund-raising lunches, brunches, dinners etc., at which *cabinet ministers would be present*, so businessmen would pay inflated prices for entry — and access to ministers — as contributions to party funds--eligible, of course, for tax breaks.

This third technique has brought in the big bucks for the QLP since 1984-85. In the 1988 fund-raising year, such "social activities," with the presence of cabinet ministers, accounted for 80 per cent of all funds raised — of a total of over $9millions.

The PQ after the September 1989 election was simply not a major party. It didn't have the resources a major party must have. In that campaign, the Liberal party spent up to the limit it was legally allowed (99.4 percent) — as a major party must spend 90 percent plus, even in defeat. What did the PQ spend on its 1989 campaign? A pitiful 56.8 percent.

The fact is that the PQ has had very few decent fund-raising years since the early 1980s (for "decent" is meant within striking distance of the QLP). Between the two elections of 1985 and 1989, the PQ raised about one-quarter of the Liberal total— and the Liberal party raised close to $30 millions total. The Liberal method was within the law and that is what counts in these matters, although the PQ complained.

Thus it is apparent that the QLP adapted to Bill 2's party financing regime in a way that is neither that of a mass party, which it appears to have done in its first years under this regime, until 1984. But the QLP has not attempted to return to its cadre party system, but found a technique between the two, which I have called a "mass/cadre" party.[188]

Meanwhile, it seems that until recently the PQ insisted on holding onto "popular" financing, to its distinct monetary loss, even while in power.

The PQ was indignant about the QLP's technique, and squarely called it "influence-peddling." If not illegal, as the DGE declared after an investigation, the QLP's major fund-raising technique *is* essentially unfair, as no opposition party can use it. It relies on the presence of cabinet ministers at functions, whose promises to businessmen are at least implied, if not firm.

But by the measure of politics, (success/failure) the Liberal technique was a huge success, while the PQ languished in dismal failure. "Much can happen and we must remember that this Liberal technique is essentially a government-party one. Should the Liberals lose power, they will have lost their key. And, since 1960, no provincial government in

Québec has had more than two mandates It will be up to the Liberal leadership to break this sequence and have a third mandate — if they can.

Between the last two elections — 1989 and 1994 — the PQ appeared to pick up on its party financing. In the run-up to the 1994 election the PQ, or at least its leader Jacques Parizeau, took a leaf out of the QLP's book by holding a number of social activities — dinners at $1,000 a plate. The extra cash showed up in the party election expenditure and, when all the bills were in, the PQ had spent 92.2 per cent of its permitted expenditure of $7,432,306 (party campaign and all candidates). This was the first time since 1981 that the PQ spent like a major party. It paid off, as with 44.7 per cent of the vote the PQ had a majority of 77 (or 61.6 percent) of the seats.

The QLP nevertheless out-spent the PQ, in defeat, with 94.4 percent of its permitted total, a vote of 44.3 per cent, but only 47. (or 38.4 per cent) of the seats.

The QLP is a major party. Come hell or high water it spends over 90 percent of what is permitted. Now that the PQ is back in power it remains to be seen if it will develop its "social activities" technique of fund-raising. If it does, it will give the QLP a strong run in the next election. But if it does it will become a very different party.

CHAPTER 6: THE QUEBEC LIBERAL PARTY AS A MASS/CADRE PARTY

In any party-financing regime it is necessary to go beyond the letter of the law, to know what amounts are raised by the various parties, and how they are raised.

As far as one can tell the PQ has always, until recently, been faithful to its original method — basically the annual door-to-door drive. But the QLP has not been so faithful to a mass method. This first caught my attention in the late 1980s, when it did not seem possible that the QLP could raise such large amounts by the traditional methods of a mass party.

Let us explore this phenomenon now. The QLP was a cadre party until the PQ government's Bill 2 in 1977. It was then reorganized, under its new leader Claude Ryan (1978-83) into a mass party for its financing. It remained in this state until it resumed power in December 1985. (The new leader, Robert Bourassa, took over in 1983). It has since, while remaining basically a mass party in its fund-raising, added an element of cadre-party fund-raising, which has given it its rather inflated fund-raising totals.

Having passed through the experience of re-election (in September 1989) the QLP found the relative simplicity and greater efficiency of the cadre-party method so convincing that it used its cadre-party technique overwhelmingly to raise funds and so could properly be termed a "mass/cadre" party. Nevertheless, the cadre party technique raised the bulk of its funds.

It seems necessary to define these terms, at least briefly: mass party, cadre party, and the composite "mass/cadre" party, the title of this chapter. Essentially, as defined by Duverger[189] these terms refer to the fund-raising practices of political parties. The cadre is the original type of party in a democracy, and is still the dominant type in many countries. Its essential financing is provided by a small number of large, or very large, donations from corporations or individuals associated with corporations.[190]

The mass party arose as a reaction to the funding method and large resources of cadre parties and also because these mass parties either could not or would not obtain large donations from business corporations. The fund-raising method is therefore based on a mass membership, as many as possible, to both contribute money (dues) and to supplement these contributions with other contributions solicited by members.

Duverger calls this method "the democratic method compared to the capitalist method." It involves many small contributions from as many people as possible, as compared to the capitalist method of donations from a few bankers, industrialists, etc.

In Quebec, the PQ was the first successful utilizer of this mass method and was Quebec's (and also perhaps Canada's) first true and successful mass party.[191] Réné Levesque in 1968 had good reasons for choosing this form of financing and organization for his new party.[192]

What is a "mass/cadre" party? This writer coined the expression to describe the funding method of the Quebec Liberal Party from 1981. In this context it indicates a party which was a mass party but which has adopted cadre party methods of fund-raising. As far as one can tell, the QLP is the only such party in Canada. This is due to the special circumstances deriving from Bill 2. No other province has similar legislation and, of course, the federal Act does not.

The QLP was accounted the second mass party in Quebec. This was at first a matter of necessity — of conforming to the law. In 1977 the PQ government enacted its party financing legislation, Bill 2, based on its own party regulations.[193] Since this law, which makes relatively small, individual contributions the only legal form of party fund acquisition, the Quebec provincial party system has contained two mass parties and, at various times, a dozen or more would-be parties. These must become mass parties to survive. The two major parties are: (1) the Parti Québecois (PQ), which seems to be a true mass party and (2) the Quebec Liberal Party (QLP), a mass party in its membership and, apparently, only in part of its financing. All minor parties (of which there were eleven in the 1985 election) have either not been able to take off, or have disappeared, or have been on the brink of disappearance, because of inability to pay debts. This high mortality rate of parties is explained, at least in part, as due to the financing regime established by Bill 2 in 1977.

This writer approached the problem of the "mass/cadre" party by two methods in two papers.[194] The first paper is based on a data set of amounts raised annually and amounts raised in "social activities." The second paper is based on a data set of amounts raised annually and amounts raised in contributions of over $100. In both papers the QLP totals are compared with the PQ. In the second data set we see some startling results.

My papers had the temerity to *add* a category to Duverger's classic categories. But the QLP had not functioned as a mass party for very long — from 1978 at the earliest until 1984 or 1985. Why does this party not revert to its pre-1978 state of cadre party? Of course the law, made by the previous (PQ) government, bars the acceptance of contributions from corporations, unions or any association. In fact, a contribution may legally be given only by an individual — a Quebec elector — and from his own personal property. Tax breaks are given for such contributions and there is a limit.

But from 1985 to 1994 the Liberal party was the party of government. Why therefore did it not change or even repeal the law? Here we touch on a matter of some delicacy. Bill 2 is a very popular law and the Liberals were doing extremely well with it. They honoured the letter of it — more or less — and not its spirit. In addition, when this party — under the same Premier Bourassa — was thrown out of office in 1976, it was under a heavy cloud of scandal, much of it connected to its fund-raising practises. No doubt, the premier would not have liked to revive those old memories. So what we have in Quebec is a law, unique in Canada, whose spirit is that all parties shall raise their funds in the manner of a mass party.[195] .However, the QLP, apparently while still in opposition in 1984, but a government in waiting, found a fund-raising technique far more efficient and requiring much less organization than the PQ's door-to-door method. This is the by-now well-known technique of organizing "social activities" of all kinds. The special Liberal wrinkle is that for all these activities it is advertised that cabinet ministers will be present. And not just present, but for those (presumably businessmen) who make a $500, $1,000 and up contribution, there will be special attention from the ministers.

Is this "influence peddling"? In opposition the PQ said it was. But the DGE investigated and found no illegality. There are plenty of unsubstantiated rumours and it is possible that there will be a juicy scandal breaking around this system. Too many people know about it and are in on it.

Although the QLP cannot accept cheques like the $50,000 one which the Canadian Pacific corporation regularly donates to both the federal Liberal and Conservative parties, still it has been well supplied with funds by its method.

THE LIBERAL SYSTEM

There is at least a difference of nuance, it seems, between the description of mass party financing by Duverger and the financing activities of the PQ — and the QLP since 1978. The nuance is that these two Quebec parties add to their members fees (which are a low), the contributions solicited by their members in an at least annual fund drive. Since the membership fees themselves have constituted a rather small proportion of totals collected, most of their money must derive from other sources.

It is apparent that membership dues in these Quebec parties, contrary to the mass parties of Europe, do not play a large role in their financing. For example, the PQ collected $411,000 in "adhesions" (memberships) in 1984. The QLP raised as much as $950,000 in memberships in 1985, but in 1988, when a fund-raising total of over $8 millions was achieved, there was only $568,000 in memberships. In Europe, on the other hand, the bulk of fund-raising is from membership dues.

So the nuance added to Duverger's description is that these two Quebec parties derive the majority of their funds from the members activities in soliciting on fund drives and not from their fees. The contributions solicited by their members constitute the *main* portion of the funds raised by the PQ since its foundation. Has it so constituted the major portion for the QLP? Let us test the QLP in the period since 1984 — a benchmark year, since in the following one the QLP returned to power.

No doubt the QLP did well in its mass fund-raising in 1984 by sheer inertia. The excitement of having a new/old leader could not have hurt either. But in 1985 the party was already heavily into "cadre" methods of social activities attended by (prospective) cabinet ministers, as shown by the figures for that fund-raising year.

After the December 1985 election the QLP numbers take off, both total fund-raising and proportion raised by social activities, as well as "proportion raised in contributions over $100," until in 1988 over 80 percent of the funds raised for the QLP are through the method of social events patronised by ministers.

As we will see in Table IV, in 1988 the QLP raised $6.14 millions in contributions over $100, and only $1.1 million in contributions under, while the PQ collected $64,840 in over-$100 contributions, and $63,760 in contributions under. Therefore, it may well be justified to term the QLP of 1985-1994, no longer a mass party, but a mass/cadre party, something quite different, in which the majority of its funds is collected by the cadre technique.

As mass parties it appeared in 1988 that "the main fund-raising method of the PQ and the QLP is to organise volunteer-members (in French "militants") to go "door-to-door to solicit relatively small contributions for the party."[196]

But in the light of experience in the following two fund-raising years, and collateral evidence, it seems clear that the QLP had not been mainly financed by this method — and had not been since 1985, when it became the government again. Instead, the party's major fund-raising method was to organise *functions* (social activities).

Such functions net thousands of dollars for the party's funds, some as much as $100,000, and hundreds of them are mounted by the QLP annually. Manifestly, this is a more efficient fund-raising method than going door-to-door for contributions which are much smaller — $20 or $50, when they are given at all.

Of course, only a party in power is able to use this method to its full effectiveness. It is not like any normal method of mass party financing, for mass parties were not in power and their militants (and some of their top brass or ministers) would not cosy up to businessmen, whom they regarded as their natural enemies. The QLP technique is more like the traditional types of government-party financing: toll-gating, or even the traditional Québec system of "kickbacks" or, in French "ristournes". It is difficult to say whether the PQ practised such a method when in power from 1976-85. Apart from the absence of Liberal accusations, the low PQ fund-raising totals in 1984 and 1985 seem to indicate that there was nothing very efficient about their fund-raising then.[197]

Yet the QLP maintained the membership totals associated with the mass, and not needed by a cadre party. In 1987 it had 161,208.[198]

This is certainly a remarkably high figure for a "non-ideological" former cadre party, especially in a non-election year. It was more than double the PQ membership that year.

The relative poverty of the PQ organization at our benchmark of 1984 can be measured by its low expenditure in the election campaign ending on December 2, 1985, as seen in Table II. This is coming off a nine-year mandate during which government-parties normally fill their coffers.

We see from Table III that the QLP has had great success in its fund-raising since 1985, while the PQ has not. Yet, the very success of the former party since it returned to power in 1985, and the failure (at least relative) of the latter raises questions about the Bill 2 regime. It appears that the QLP's success in the past four years was out of all proportion to anything achieved by the PQ.

Yet in the two years before the latest election, 1992-94, PQ fund-raising quickened. In 1993-94 the PQ actually raised a larger amount than the QLP, unprecedented since the early 1980s. The only changed features in the PQ effort was a new sense of trying, and the social activities. On the other side was the poorest QLP total in years. The combination was enough to power the PQ to victory on September 12, 1994.

TABLE III

Party Expenditures in the Quebec Election of Dec. 2, 1985

Party	Party Expenditure	Permitted Expenditure	Percentage Col. 1 of 2
	$	$	%
PQ	826,658	1,144,150	72.2
QLP	1,132,797	1,144,150	99.0

Source: Director General of Elections, Quebec 85. Summaries of reports of election expenses (Québec 1986) p.3

TABLE IV

FUND-RAISING TOTALS (LESS SUBSIDY)

			Total raised in donations over $100		Percentage of cols. 4 & 5 by cols. 2 & 3	
YEAR	PQ	QLP	PQ	QLP	PQ	QLP
1984	$2.1M	$4.9M	$0.04M	$1.9M	0.02%	38.8%
1985	$4.0M	$9.0M	$0.7M	$5.0M	0.14%	55.6%
1986	$6.9M	$10.0M	$N/A	N/A	-----	-----
1987	$2.0M	$8.8M	N/A	N/A	-----	-----
1988	$1.7M	$8.9M	0.06M	$6.6M	0.35%	68.5%
1989	$3.8M	$4.6M	0.4M	$2.8M	0.11%	60.9%
1990	$2.5M	$5.9M	0.12M	$4.3M	0.05%	72.9%

SOURCES: DGE Quebec, *RAPPORTS FINANCIERS* (Quebec: Official Publisher 1984-1990). *NOTE*: There are various ways given by these reports of calculating a party's total fund-raising in a year. The annual report requires categories of: (1) total raised in donations over $100; (2) total in less than $100 donations; (3) membership fees; (4) admissions & registrations; (5) anonymous contributions; (6) subsidies from the DGE; (7) transfers from other elements of the party (8) other revenues.

For purposes of Table IV, I have chosen to accept all of these categories as valid fund-raising except the subsidies received through the Director General, which is a matter of automatic law. For these two parties the subsidy (only *they* currently receive it) amounts to about $600,000 per annum.

Table IV shows the fund-raising fortunes of the two major provincial parties of Quebec from 1984 to 1990. 1984 was chosen as a benchmark as it was the year before the PQ left office (in the 1985 election) and when the QLP assumed it. The first two columns are the totals raised, minus the government subsidy, and the third and fourth columns are the totals raised in donations of over $100 each. The final two columns show the percentages raised by such donations.

The point is that while in the first paper on this topic ("The QLP as a mass/cadre party") I concentrated on the amounts raised in "social activities, in the second paper ("Duverger Revisited: The Mass/Cadre Party") I focused on the totals raised in donations of over $100. If the last two columns of Table IV are examined, we see that its percentages for the PQ are nothing short of pitiful, ranging from 0.02 per cent in 1984, when they were still in power, to 0.14 per cent in 1985, 0.035 percent in 1988, 0.11 percent in 1989 and 0.05 percent in 1990. Unfortunately, the data for 1986 and 1987 are not available.

Yet the Liberals, even in 1984, before taking power, had 38.8 percent of their total raised in these relatively large amounts. In 1985 their percentage jumped to 55.6 per cent, in 1988 to 68.5 per cent, 1989 to 60.9 per cent and in 1990 to 72.9 per cent.

But it is the pairing of these dyads which is very telling and is actually really hard to believe. After all, these are two major parties in a single system. But these parties do not match at all. If we pair them: in 1984 the PQ has $0.04 million raised in amounts of over $100, so that it barely computes, 0.02 per cent, while the QLP opposition party raises 38.8 percent of its total ($4.9 millions) this way. 1985 PQ 0.14 percent; QLP 55.6 percent. 1988 PQ 0.35 percent; QLP 68.5 percent. 1989 PQ 0.11 percent; QLP 60. 9 percent. 1990 PQ 0.05 percent; QLP 72.9 percent.

It is hard to imagine a set of figures which said so clearly that one party is the master of fund-raising and the other is not. Obviously it is the QLP which dominated in this area. This data set means, it seems, that it was the QLP which collected the bigger donations — and more of them.

We have emphasized this data set, by repeating it, because it seems quite amazing. It seems that one major party averaged about 60 per- cent of the available supply and the other less than ten percent; this is not simply unusual but extraordinary.

There is, by the way, no finite number (100 per cent) of $100 plus donations. It's just a question of how many were given to the parties in a single year. The percentages in Table IV are from the amounts given in donations of $100 plus to the total raised for the year.

Contributions of over $100 are likely to be from businessmen. So, apart from the current story that businessmen give a bonus or other amount of money to executives, or other employees, on the understanding that they will donate it to the boss's favourite party. [199] This is clearly illegal, for the law specifies that the donation must be from the elector's (donor's) own personal property. But the dealings between ministers and other government officials and businessmen seem to be the main conduit for the QLP's record-breaking fund-raising since 1985. And the apparent reluctance to use them the main reason for the PQ's poor fund-raising performance.

Thus we see in Table IV (Columns 3 and 4) that the QLP collected the big bucks (donations over $100) while the PQ has had to eke out its meagre totals with relatively small contributions.

We cannot expect a design, such as Duverger's of Political party financing — so succinct and elegant — to cover all possible eventualities. Once before I had occasion to add a sub-category, which I termed the "Administrative" party.[200] The party under examination was Quebec's Union Nationale, the government-party from 1936-39 and also from 1944-60 and from 1966-70. It is now extinct — extinguished by the DGE in 1989 for non-payment of its debts.

The Union Nationale[201] certainly exploited its position in power as a true cadre party. In spite of its being a "nationalist" party and thus anathema to nearly all English-speaking Canadians, it is documented as having regularly received a cadre party's large donations from the corporations, whose business elite controlled Quebec's economy.[203]

A student wrote in a research paper for me: "Nationalist parties, prior to the Quiet Revolution, were never well financed as all the money was in English hands." Well, I would say that would depend on whether your party was Sauvé's Nationalists of 1927 or Duplessis' Union Nationale. It might depend also on how "Nationalist" was defined.

The great "Administrative" parties of this century (Taschereau and Duplessis) also had a large element of what can only be called "self-financing." This ranged from toll-gating, the quasi-sale of permits and licences for party donations and, in sum, it was the government and its administration that served to pour large amounts into the party's coffers. Thus the appellation of "Administrative" party, which is not found in Duverger's categories.

It seemed that Duverger had taken cognizance of these "Administrative" parties — but as archaic. He seems to do this elsewhere in his study than in the main Party-financing passages.[203]

The subject of my two papers[204] is a different kind of party that could not have been brought under Duverger's categories. At least for Quebec it involves specific legislation to make the full cadre party impossible, and to encourage the mass party financing system for example, tax breaks for small contributions. Until recently the PQ steadfastly clung not only to a mass party technique, but also to the techniques it pioneered and made work in Quebec from its foundation in 1968. The QLP, on the other hand, has sought out a technique of fund-raising to supplement what it could raise by the mass method — and made a smashing success of what may be called the "mass/cadre" party technique.

Let us examine the QLP's fund-raising techniques more closely:
The "Evening with a Minister" is the most profitable of the three current
Quebec Liberal techniques. Then-QLP Director General John Parisella
said that there are ministers who "bring out as much as $1,000 for the
privilege of hobnobbing with power."[205] "Slightly less profitable" is
Technique No. 2, which is to go through lists of members (the list is
usually over 100,000) and contact those "due" for another contribution.
Technique No. 3 (the least profitable) "hit and miss, door-to-door fund
drive."

The QLP's success from 1984-94 has been out of all proportion to
anything achieved by the PQ even when that party was in power from
1976 to 1985. Attendance at the QLP's social activities was largely by
businessmen, and though PQ charges of influence peddling may not be
sustainable in court, and though the businessman's contribution to QLP
funds cannot amount to the old cadre party donations of pre-1977[206] still,
their contributions, for admissions of $500 or $1,000, are substantially
greater than an average contribution of $20 or $50, which used to be
normal in the two parties' fund drives in the years after 1977. They may
still be for the PQ, but in the Liberal campaigns some give the maximum
annual gift of $3,000.

If the PQ could utilize a similar technique there would be an element
of equity. But the key element of the Liberals' social activities is the
presence of — and access to — cabinet ministers. Obviously, this makes
this technique unavailable to any but a government-party, or one close to
power. How much will a businessman pay for access to an opposition
critic?

In defence of the QLP's main technique, one could say: What's wrong
with a businessman renting a minister and donating the price of the
rental to the minister's party fund? He can tell him his troubles and what
he would like the government to do about them. There is nothing wrong.
It is, in effect, what ministers actually *do* a lot of the time. However, if
the minister promises to do anything for the businessman, or if he
promises him a government contract, that is an offence called "influence-
peddling." The PQ said Liberal ministers committed this offence
constantly. One particular incident that came to light is the charge by
André Boulerice (PQ-St. Jacques). On May 2, 1989:[207]

> he tabled an invitation from some paving and construction contractors to
> a Liberal fund-raising golf competition, which mentions the entry fee of
> $1,000, as well as the participation in the tournament of Tourism Minister
> Michel Gratton, Agriculture Minister Michel Page — and Marc Yvan
> Cote who, as Minister of Transport, was responsible for building and
> repairing roads, in which paving and construction contractors have an
> avid interest.

Boulerice told the Assembly that the companies of contractors who sent the invitation received contracts from the Liberal government worth more than $26 millions since 1985.

CONCLUSION TO CHAPTER SIX

In these two complementary papers I tried to describe what seems largely the reality of the QLP's fund-raising since 1984. In the former paper ("The QLP as a Mass/Cadre Party") I concentrated on the totals raised by the QLP in "social activities" directly. In the second paper ("Duverger Revisited: The Mass/ Cadre Party") I have supplemented this with an analysis of the totals raised by donations of over $100 each. Both of these analyses seem to fit the suppositions of its thesis well.

As a well-oiled fund-raising machine the QLP seemed virtually to be selling contracts and favours of other kinds. Did its system reach the degree of efficiency and routinization of fund-raising of some government parties in the voluminous literature? We cannot know until a commission may probe its practices, as did the Salvas Commission those of the Union Nationale government-party from 1955-60 (1963).

Probably the Bourassa government covered its tracks better than those uncovered by the Cliche Commission in the late 1970s. In the case of the Salvas or Cliche Commissions the scale would certainly be smaller. A $3,000 contribution to Duplessis' Union Nationale might be considered as "small potatoes." But still, this QLP technique is simple, relatively easy to organise and, although it cannot raise the kind of money Duplessis did, does raise much more than what seems to be the PQ's strictly mass method.

It thus certainly seems justifiable to conclude that the QLP was no longer a mass party, if it ever was, but became a composite type, the "mass/cadre" party.

CHAPTER 7: CONCLUDING CHAPTER

From the beginning of the Quiet Revolution there seem to have been few Quebec leaders who wanted to follow in Taschereau's or Duplessis' footsteps of the "occult" or slush fund. More had ambitions to eliminate it. Jean Lesage in 1965 cited his Bill 15 as an example of his government's plans to eliminate the system of political slush funds by limiting expenses and helping candidates. Claude Ryan was well known for his detestation of slush funds. Of the use of Bill 15 in the 1966 election he said: "Secret election funds were not entirely absent, but occult financing was not a major factor." Finally, we know from Graham Fraser[208] that Réné Levesque particularly hated the slush fund system. His experience in the Lesage cabinet was enough, it appears, to give him this feeling. In addition, his experience in Europe (with the US army) gave him a feeling for the European mass party. Still, with all this taken into account, it was not likely that a social-democratic, *indépendantiste* Quebec party would receive any donations from Quebec's (still) Anglo corporate elite.

Quebec's traditional party-financing system was transformed by Bill 15 in 1963, and still more by Bill 2 in 1977. Bill 15 and subsequent direct subsidies assisted the finances of the major parties, and the reimbursements to candidates assist the major parties most, but other candidates could benefit if they get 20 percent of the vote. All of this was of some financial assistance, overwhelmingly to the two major parties (until the 1970 election these were the Liberal party and the Union Nationale).

But Bill 2 transformed the Quebec party financing system, although not quite as had been expected, we see now. With its experience in "popular" financing, gained since its foundation in 1968, the PQ, assisted by its wave of popularity until the economic recession in 1981, as expected, out-raised the QLP, which was just organising its mass funding system.

But, after the PQ virtually self-destructed between 1981 and 1985, with a loss of popularity — quite remarkable — this led to a reduction in funds raised. The QLP, under Bourassa from 1983, developed the fund-raising technique described in Chapter Six. The statistics show that this system really took off, both in amounts raised, proportion due to "social activities" and proportion in donations over $100, in 1985. For while the election was not until December, yet for that whole year the QLP was seen as a "government-in-waiting."

While in office the QLP perfected its system, and although the total raised has not been larger every year, still it has never fallen much. And in 1988, the pre-election year, the total raised was startling, and 80 per cent of it was raised through the main technique described — of social activities.

Now that the PQ is back in office (1994) it is possible that some kind of fund-raising parity can be achieved between these two major parties. It seems that the PQ will have to make some radical changes to its fund-raising system. As for the QLP, the kind of loss of popularity leading to a reduction in contributions, as is described for the PQ elsewhere,[186] should not affect the QLP as much, financially, since its main technique does not rely as much on its popularity with its contributing businessmen. It seems likely that there will be a drought in QLP finances, without ministers to put on show at fund-raising functions. It remains to be seen if Premier Parizeau presses his will in "social activities" for fund-raising. He used the technique in the run-up to the 1994 election, but will he depart so far from the PQ's tradition as to "routinize" the technique? It is a very tempting option.

EPILOGUE — 1993-94

The latest election took place on September 12, 1994. In this election the provincial electorate seemed to have declared its intention on becoming an independent country, separate from Canada. But the vote was very close: 44.7 percent for the leading Parti Quebecois (and 77 seats, or 61.6%of the 125) to 44.3 per cent for the out-going Liberals (and 47 seats, or 38.4 percent of them). So the accession to independence will depend on the results of a referendum to be held probably in the fall of 1995.

The closeness of the result was matched by the two parties' fund-raising over the period previous to the election on September 12, 1994. In 1989 the Liberal party spent, in its campaign for the election, $1,186,008 or 99.4 per cent of its permitted total party campaign, while the Parti Québecois spent $677,770 or 56.8 percent of its permitted total. The third party, the Equality Party, spent only 10.3 per cent of a very small total ($187,752) based on only a few candidates. Most of its campaign was conducted by the candidates. It actually spent only $19,360 and won four seats.

But the jump in the PQ's spending in 1994 is startling. For only the second time in its history it spent over 90 per cent -92.2 percent of its permitted total. The QLP, however, spent its usual major party proportion -- 94.4 percent, in defeat:

LIBERAL AND PARTI QUÉBECOIS INTER-ELECTION FUND-RAISING, 1990-1993

1990 Liberal $5.9 millions; PQ $2.3 millions
1991 Liberal $5.7 milllons; PQ $2.6 millions
1992 Liberal $3.6 millions; PQ $3.2 millions.

But in 1993--94 the PQ made a determined effort:

SOCIAL ACTIVITIES: THE PQ IMITATES THE QLP

For the first time the DGE's Report showed that the PQ has begun imitating the Liberals in fund-raising. Last year (1993) the PQ held 10 such activities at which it raised a total of $203,800. These included six dinners at $2,000 a plate, which the Report indicates were attended by small groups of only 710 contributors, *LA PRESSE* reported that the dinners were also attended by such senior PQ officials (and prospective members of a future PQ government) as party leader Parizeau, Vice-President Bernard Landry, executive member Jean Campeau and opposition House Leader Guy Chevrette.

Even though such activities are entirely legal, they nevertheless violate the spirit of Levesque's law Bill 2. Who says so? Why, the PQ itself. Or at least that's what it said five years ago, when the PQ opposition in the Assembly was attacking the Liberals for charging a $1,000 entry fee for a golf tournament and advertising the presence of three Liberal cabinet ministers.

But when the PQ was poised to take power itself, it discovered how profitable it can be to sell a few hours with future senior ministers to anyone who has a pet project to push — and, of course, a couple of thousand bucks in disposable cash to be remembered by.

Quebec's main political parties were in good financial shape and ready to do battle in the 1994 provincial election, according to the DGE, Pierre-F. Côté.

Mr. Côté gave Quebec's political system a clean bill of health in the release of his financial report for 1993. He told a news conference: "I think the Liberal party and the Parti Québecois have enough money to run a good campaign."

PQ leader Jacques Parizeau said that if his party turns its lead in the polls into an election victory, he will likely hold a referendum to separate from Canada next year.

The figures showed that the Liberals of Premier Daniel Johnson had a much larger war chest than the PQ. As of December 31, 1993, the Liberals had about $4.7 millions on hand while the PQ had about $1.6 million.

But the parties had been collecting money since the beginning of the year with an eye to the coming election campaign. The PQ announced earlier in May 1994 that it collected $3.3 millions in this year's fund-raising campaign. The Liberals had not yet announced the results of their campaigns but are expected to meet their goal of $4.3 millions. Mr. Côté added that the parties will be under strict spending limits of about $7.2 millions each for the campaign (this includes the party campaign and all the candidates). Half of that amount is repaid by the provincial treasury (in reimbursements to candidates). The subsidies to the two major parties in 1994 amounted to $2.3M for the QLP and $2.2M for the PQ-together 91.4 percent of the total subsidy.

TABLE V
Permitted Election Expenses of Major Parties & Their Declared Expenditures at Quebec General Elections 1966--1989

Parties	Permited Expenses	Expendi-tures	Expenditures as % of Permitted
1966 General Election			
Union Nationale	797,757	588,666	73.8%
Liberal Party	797,757	688,288	86.3%
Totals 1966:	**2,923,015**	**1,309,575**	**44.8%**
1970 General Election			
Union Nationale	849,528	778,545	91.6%
Liberal Party	849,528	827,341	97.4%
Parti Québecois	849,528	265,994	31.3%
Totals 1970:	**3,465,058**	**1,963,501**	**56.7%**
1973 General Election			
Union Nationale	907,246	613,861	67.7%
Liberal Party	907,246	854,018	94.1%
Parti Québecois	907,246	402,204	44.3%
Totals 1973:	**3,740,709**	**2,148,935**	**57.5%**
1976 General Election			
Union Nationale	970,394	464,387	47.9%
Liberal Party	986,618	963,564	97.7&
Parti Québecois	986,618	757,389	76.8%
Totals 1976:	**4,801,867**	**2,384,187**	**49.7%**
1981 General Election			
Liberal Party	1,079,222	1,062,561	98.5%
Parti Québecois	1,079,222	1,049,138	97.2%
1981 Totals:	**2,158,444**	**2,111,619**	**97.8%**
1985 General Election			
Liberal Party	1,144,150	1,132,796	99.0%
Parti Québecois	1,144,150	826,658	72.2%
Totals 1985:	**2,288,300**	**1,959,454**	**85.6%**

Table cont'd...
1989 General Election

Liberal Party	1,192,878	1,186,008	99.4%
Parti Québecois	1,192,878	677,770	56.8%
Totals 1989:	**2,385,756**	**1,863,778**	**78.1%**

SOURCES: All numbers, except percentages, are based on *REPORTS* (Election Expenses) of either the President général des élections 1967, 1971, 1974, or of the Directeur général des élections 1978, 1982, 1986 and 1990.

1) Dollar totals are rounded to the nearest dollar. 2) The Director General of Elections of Quebec, M. Pierre-F. Côté, criticized this Table for including only party campaign expenditures and no expenditures by major party candidates. I would say to him that it is an open scandal in Quebec that nearly all the candidates of the two major parties are guaranteed partial reimbursement, no matter how few votes they get. Everywhere else every candidate must get some votes to be reimbursed. My colleague Louis Massicotte calls this Quebec rule a "giant fraud".

TABLE VI
LIBERAL & PARTI QUÉBECOIS FUNDRAISING 1983*--1992

YEAR	LIBERAL (millions $)	PARTI QUÉBECOIS (millions $)
1983	2.1	2.1
1984	4.9	2.0
1985+	9.0	2.3
1986	10.1	0.9
1987	8.8	1.0
1988	8.9	1.6
1989+	4.6	2.0
1990	5.9	2.3
1991	5.7	2.6
1992	3.6	3.2

* Last change of government was in 1985.
+ Election year.

SOURCES: Liberal amounts from *RAPPORTS FINANCIERS*,
Directeur général des élections for the year indicated. Parti Québecois,
Document Campagne de financement, from Permanence Nationale,
Danielle Rioux, n.d.

1) The DGE also takes me to task for using figures from a PQ
Campagne de financement document, rather than his party
RAPPORTS FINANCIERS. Part of the trouble is that his RAPPORTS
are so confusing that I cannot trust any figure that I get from them.

The DGE also complains that I did not take into account the
expenses incurred in fund-raising,

AFTERWORD

In the 1993--94 fund-raising year, the Parti Québecois leader, Jacques Parizeau, finally caved in to his party's "realist" fund-raisers. He allowed the holding of fund-raising dinners at $1,000 per plate, for the first time. This was no doubt responsible for the party's startlingly high expenditures in the September 12, 1994 provincial election. Only once before had the PQ spent over 90 percent of its permitted expenditure--and that was in 1981, with the PQ in power for five years. The high-ticket fund-raising social activity is a method that PQ leaders said they would never employ. Until Parizeau, they were all attached to "popular financing" that is, the door-to-door solicitation of small contributions.

Will this successful experiment be repeated now that the PQ is back in power, and have Ministers to appear at such activities? If so, it will mark the beginning of another mass/cadre party in Quebec. The method that was so heavily criticized by the PQ when the Liberals were so successful with it will become their own. And the Liberals? The recent relative paucity of their fund-raising, even before they lost the election, seems to indicate a period of drought for them.

ENDNOTES

INTRODUCTION

1. M.D. Behiels, *PRELUDE TO THE QUIET REVOLUTION: LIBERALISM VERSUS NEO-NATIONALISM 1945-60* (Kingston & .Montreal: McGill-Queen's University Press, 1985)
2. H. Guindon, "Social Unrest, Social Class & Quebec's Bureaucratic Revolution" first published in *QUEEN'S QUARTERLY: SUMMER 1964* and several times thereafter.
3. See H.M. Angell, "Le financement des partis politiques provinciaux québecois" Chapter 2 in *PERSONNEL ET PARTIS POLITIQUES AU QUEBEC*, V. Lemieux, ed (Montreal: Boreal Express, 1982)
4. B.L. Vigod, *QUEBEC BEFORE DUPLESSIS: THE POLITICAL CAREER OF LOUIS-ALEXANDRE TASCHEREAU* (Kingston & Montreal: McGill-Queen's University Press, 1986)
5. For a recent assessment of party financing in France, see C. Landfried, "Money & Politics in France" ECPR, Paris, paper presented April 1989.
6. L. Massicotte, "Une reforme inachevée: Les règles du jeu électoral, *RECHERCHES SOCIOGRAPHIQUES*, XXV:1, 1984, 81.
7. *REPORT OF THE COMMITTEE ON ELECTION EXPENSES / RAPPORT DU COMITÉ DES DÉPENSES ÉLECTORALES* & accompanying volume: *STUDIES IN CANADIAN PARTY FINANCE / ÉTUDES DU FINANCEMENT DES PARTIS POLITIQUES CANADIENS* (Ottawa: Queen's Printer, 1966).
8. Massicotte 43-81.
9. R.S.Q., c. F-2.
10. Maurice Duverger, *Les partis politiques* (Paris: Armand Colin, 1951). Version used here is 3rd English edition, translated by Barbara & Robert North, *POLITICAL PARTIES* (London: Methuen, 1963). Also used L.D. Epstein, *POLITICAL PARTIES IN WESTERN DEMOCRACIES* (New York: Praeger,1967).

11. Duverger, 59, 63-65, 73-76.
12. Later premier S.N. Parent is a perfect example of this type when Taschereau first meets him as an aspirant to a legislative career. He (Taschereau) becomes a "Parentiste" and rockets upwards from that point. Parent owned key things (and was Mayor) in Quebec City. Vigod, 45-6 et seq.
13. Firm figures for such contributions are hard to come by. But R.O. Sweezey for the Beauharnois Power Company revealed to the Parliamentary Committee that his donation to the federal Liberal party was $700,000. I do not claim that this was a representative contribution, but I will say that such "business" contributions to political parties were in the tens of thousands rather than in the thousands.
14. See H.M. Angell, "The Evolution & Application of Quebec Election Expense Legislation 1960-66." Study No. 7 in *REPORT OF THE COMMITTEE ON ELECTION EXPENSES* (Ottawa: Queen's Printer, 1966) 279-319.
15. Reg Whitaker, *THE GOVERNMENT PARTY: ORGANIZING & FINANCING THE LIBERAL PARTY OF CANADA 1930-58* (Toronto: University of Toronto Press, 1977).
16. K.Z. Paltiel, *POLITICAL PARTY FINANCING IN CANADA* (Toronto: McGraw-Hill, 1970).

CHAPTER ONE

17. Duverger, *POLITICAL PARTIES*, 59, 63-65, 73-76.
18. Until 1964 the *federal* Liberal party in Quebec and the *provincial* Liberal party were a single and same organization. This *organization* worked for the *Liberal party*, whether in provincial or federal politics, and the sources of funds were the same. Thus when a writer talks of the Liberal party in Quebec before 1964 it is organizationally indistinguishable as between federal and provincial, especially in financing.
19. *QUEBEC BEFORE DUPLESSIS.*
20. Vigod, frontispiece.
21. Ibid, ix.
22. 1. The term "Le roi negre" was used by Andre Laurendeau, *LE DEVOIR*, July 4, 1958. 2. The colonization idea was used in

Leandre Bergeron's *A PATRIOT'S HISTORY OF QUEBEC* (Toronto: New Canada, 1971).. 3. The longevity thesis was in my own thesis "*QUEBEC PROVINCIAL POLITICS IN THE 1920s*" (McGill M.A. thesis unpublished, 1960) based on H.F. Quinn, *THE UNION NATIONALE: A STUDY IN QUEBEC NATIONALISM* (Toronto: University of Toronto Press, 1963) In general Michel Brunet, *LA PRÉSENCE ANGLAISE ET LES CANADIENS* (P.E. Trudeau, "Some Obstacles to Democracy in Quebec" *CJEPS*, 24, Aug. 1958, J. & M. Hamelin, *LES MOEURS ELECTORALES AU QUÉBEC* (Eds du Jour, 1962), M. Durocher, "Le long regne de Duplessis: Un essai d'explication" *RHAF*? 25 December 1971, R. Heintzman "Image & Consequences" JOURNAL OF CANADIAN STUDIES 13, Summer 1978, whose full comment (in footnote 2) is that "Taschereau is but 'a Duplessis with better manners; corrupt, self-serving, allied to forces of reaction in matters economic, cultural and spiritual'."

23. Vigod, x.
24. Ibid, 13.
25. Parent himself, as Mayor of Quebec City, forced a company to build a St. Lawrence bridge, and was a director of the Quebec Railway, Light & Power Co. He became Premier later.
26. Ibid, 35. Ibid,
27. 76. See L. Bergeron *A HISTORY OF QUEBEC: A PATRIOT'S HANDBOOK* (Toronto: New Canada, 1971) 171.
28. Vigod, 84.
28. Ibid, 96.
30. Ibid, 98.
31. Ibid, 100.
32. Ibid, 101.
33. Ibid, 105.
34. Ibid, 107.
35. Ibid, 108.
36. See H.M. Angell, "Le système électorale québecois" Chapter XX in *LE SYSTEME POLITIQUE DU CANADA: INSTITUTIONS FÉDERALES ET QUÉBECOISES* (Ottawa: Les Éditions de l'Université d'Ottawa, 1968) 287-301 .
37. *ANNUAIRE DU QUÉBEC* (Quebec Yearbook) 1974.

38. The best example in Quebec is the 1973 election, when the Liberals won 102 of the 110 seats available, or 92.7 percent of the seats, for only 54.7 percent of the votes-- a disparity of +38 points.

39. Robert Rumilly, *HISTOIRE DE LA PROVINCE DU QUÉBEC*, 41, vols. (Montreal: various publishers, 1940-69). Cited hereafter as *HPQ*. This note 29:19. See Vigod, 137.

40. Ibid, 137.

41. Ibid. 142 based on *LE MONDE OUVRIER* 7, 14 mai 1927.

42. Ibid, 143.

43. Ibid, 154.

44. Ibid, 127.

45. David H. Fischer, *LE SOLEIL*, 28 July 1929 in Vigod, 128.

46. H.B. Neatby, *WILLIAM LYON MACKENZIE KING*, Vols. 2 & 3, *THE LONELY HEIGHTS* (Toronto: Macmillan, 1963-77, 375-85; N. Ward, ed *A PARTY POLITICIAN: THE MEMOIRS OF CHUBBY POWER* (Toronto: Macmillan, 1966) 285-6, 313, 337 in Vigod, 128.

47. Ibid.

48. Ibid.

49. Supra p.18 from Vigod, ibid, 128.

50. Ibid, 129

51. Ibid

52. At least not from *Quebec Before Duplessis*.

53. Ibid, 53

54. Reg Whitaker, *THE GOVERNMENT PARTY: ORGANIZING & FINANCING THE_LIBERAL PARTY OF CANADA 1930-1958* (Toronto & Buffalo: Univ. of Toronto Press, 1977 (324).

55. Vigod, 167

56. Ibid, 1923 election—94, 100-8, 162, 253; 1927 election—138-43,145

57. T.D. Regehr, *THE BEAUHARNOIS SCANDAL: A STORY OF CANADIAN ENTREPRENEURSHIP & POLITICS* (Toronto: Univ. of Toronto Press, 1990) xi, 234. Reviewed by Joseph Wearing, *CDN JRNL POL SC.* XXIII:3 (Sep. 1990) 583-4

58. A Special Select Committee of the House of Commons revealed that a former civil servant and a Liberal Senator, who was a friend of Mackenzie King, had made huge profits through having used privileged information.

59. Whitaker, 12
60. He was Laurier's chief political ally in the Quebec City district. Ibid, Preface vii.
61. Ibid, 48
62. Ibid, 49
63. Ibid, 53
64. See Vigod, 53. It involved a struggle to control utilities in Quebec City between the Quebec Railway, Light & Power Co., controlled by Forget and Holt. The rival Liberal company was called Dorchester Electric. It retained Taschereau's law firm as solicitors.
65. Ibid, 54
66. His solicitors were Robert Taschereau, son of Alexandre's step-brother and J.L. Perron. By the early 1920's F-A. Robert controlled the Merger (the Conservative companies in Quebec City) and Perron was in the provincial Cabinet. Meanwhile, Dorchester Electric had become a Shawinigan Water & Power subsidiary called the Public Service Corp. Cannon was still leading advocate, and now related to Taschereau by marriage as well as legal partnership. Premier Lomer Gouin had joined Shawinigan's Board of Directors after leaving the premiership. Taschereau managed to remain neutral in the ensuing struggle between Liberal interests, won by the PSC. But the new monopoly, renamed the Quebec Power Co., still retained the law firm, which now included Taschereau's oldest son Paul as well as Cannon. Soon brother Edmond became a director of the QPC, while Lanctot was rumoured to enjoy a retainer from the parent company (Ibid, 54).
67. HPQ 26:196-234, in Vigod, 103
68. Prices had risen and no one cared if the Meighen (federal Conservative) government was primarily responsible. The dispossessed retailers wanted revenge and the Chairman, Simard, refused to "cooperate" with the Liberal organizers.
69. "Evidence & Report of The Special Committee on the Beauharnois Power Project" *JOURNAL OF THE HOUSE OF COMMONS*, 1931. Vigod at 74.
70. In *LE DEVOIR*, 11 août 1931.
71. Based on The King Papers. Taschereau to King, December 18, 1928; June 4, 1929. Vigod Ibid.
72. Whitaker, 12

73. R. Heintzman, "Political Culture of Quebec 1840--1960" CJPS XVI: 1, March 1 983, 3-59..

CHAPTER 2

74. *DIARY*, June 18, 1935.
75. This system as practised under the Union Nationale is fully documented by H.F. Quinn, *THE UNION NATIONALE*: Quebec Nationalism from Duplessis to Levesque, 2nd edition (Toronto: Univ. of Toronto Press, 1979) Chapter VII.
76. *THE MONTREAL STAR*, October 12, 1961, "Complainant Tells Story of Extortion".
77. (Quebec) Commission of Inquiry instituted by Order in Council No. 1621, October 5, 1960. *REPORT* of The Commission concerning the purchasing methods used in the Dept of Colonization & the Govt. Purchasing Service from July 1, 1955 to June 30, 1960. The "Salvas" Report was published at Montreal on June 27, 1963.
78. *THE MONTREAL STAR* October 4, 1961.
79. Conrad Black, (Toronto) *WEEKLY MAGAZINE*, 29:36, Sep. 8, 1979, p.4. Stories abound of capitalists like J.W. McConnell of *THE* (Montreal) *STAR* walking into Duplessis' office with a briefcase packed with banknotes "for Le Chef's good works".
80. LE DEVOIR and *THE* (Montreal) *GAZETTE*, July 13, 1936. See H.M. Angell, *QUEBEC PROVINCIAL POLITICS IN THE 1920's* (McGill University Montreal, M.A. Thesis, 1960) 195.
81. Andre Larendeau, "Avant le congrès, visitons le musée de l'Union Nationale", *LE MAGAZINE MACLEAN*, October 1961.
82. R.L. Schuyler & C.C. Weston, *BRITISH CONSTITUTIONAL HISTORY SINCE 1832* (New York: Van Nostrand, 1957) 37.
83. For the U.S. see especially V.O. Key Jr., *AMERICAN STATE POLITICS* (New York: Knopf, 1956) and *SOUTHERN POLITICS* (New York: Knopf, 1949).
84. For more detail see H.M. Angell, "Duverger, Epstein & The Problem of The Mass Party: The Case of The Parti Québecois" *CDN JRNL OF POL SCI* XX:2 (June 1987).
85. See R. Macgregor Dawson, *THE GOVERNMENT OF CANADA*, 5th edition, revised by N. Ward (Toronto: Univ. of Toronto Press, 1970) 481.

86. See infra.
87. *THE GAZETTE*, May 16, 1927.
88. Speech by Zéphirin Hébert to the Conservative Club of Montreal, reported in the *GAZETTE,* May 12, 1927. That is an example of a control which is rapid and direct, don't you think?
89. James Scott, "Political Slush Funds Corrupt, All Parties," *MACLEAN'S Magazine* (Toronto) Sept. 9, 1961. As Prof. Paltiel writes on this subject, "the influence of money contributors and collectors can only be assessed if one is prepared to dispose of the myth that no price need be paid by a political party for the acquisition of financial resources. Canadians continue to cling to the idea that campaign contributions are a private affair, a matter of secrecy, something between the giver and the party of which the public should remain ignorant. The financial history of Canadian parties, however, is singularly devoid of acts of altruism. All the evidence is to the contrary. *Material gain, policy decisions,. the choice of leaders_and the general course of govt. activity* have all been counters in the effort to provide funds for the parties. At the lowest level the price has been concessions, dispensations and specific acts of patronage; at a higher level the aim has been to 'stabilize the field for corporate activity.' In both cases contributions have assured access to other decision making authorities in party and government. K.Z. Paltiel, *POLITICAL PARTY FINANCING IN CANADA*, 161.

CHAPTER 3

143. H.M. Angell, *Report on Electoral Reform of the Province of Québec*, (MTL, QLF, 1961).
144. Committee on Election Expenses, *REPORT* (Ottawa: Queen's Printer, 1966). There was a chapter devoted to Quebec--Study No. 7, pp. 279-319, by myself. Most of what follows is from this study.
145. ELECTION ACT, RSQ, 1964, c.7, s.379 (1)
146. *LE DEVOIR* 7 dec 1956.
147. Hamelin, J. & M. *LES MOEURS ELECTORALES DANS LE QUÉBEC*, de *1791 à nos jours* (Montreal: Eds du Jour, 1962).
148. 17 & 18 Vict. 1854, c. 102.
149. THE QUEBEC ELECTION ACT, 38 Vict. 1875, c.7.

150. H.M. Angell, Study No. 7, *REPORT OF THE COMMITTEE ON ELECTION EXPENSES* (Ottawa: Queen's Printer, 1966) 282. Henceforth cited as RCOEE.

151. THE QUEBEC ELECTION ACT, 59 Vict. 1895, c. IX.

152. M. Duverger, *POLITICAL PARTIES*, 354-5.

153. But until 1970 the Créditistes acted only at the federal level. See M.B. Stein, "The Structure & Functions of the Finances of the Ralliement des Créditistes" Committee on Election Expenses, *STUDIES IN CANADIAN PARTY FINANCE* (Ottawa, Queen's Printer, 1966) 405-458.

154. We have dealt with two of them--Taschereau Chapter One and Duplessis Chapter Two.

155. For details see Chapter Two--Duplessis, supra. The "kickbacks" system was investigated by the Salvas Commission, which reported in 1963.

156. Or anywhere else. We have seen that this type of self-financing party existed widely, at least in North America, see V.O. Key, *SOUTHERN POLITICS* and *AMERICAN STATE POLITICS*, Knopf, 1956 and 1949.

157. For details see H.M. Angell, "Duverger, Epstein & The Problem of the Mass Party: The Case of the Parti Québecois, *CDN JRNL POL SCI*, XX:2 (June 1987).

158. Most of these flaws and loopholes were filled by the FEDERAL ELECTION EXPENSE ACT of 1974.

159. Montreal: Quebec Liberal Federation 1961.

160. H.M. Angell, "Party & Candidate Spending in the Quebec General Election of April 1981, unpublished.

161. *THE MONTREAL STAR*, editorial Nov.14, 1961, p. 10

162. Rapport du 7e Congrès annuel, la Federation Libérale du Québec, 60-64. Full English translation in Angell, "Research Study", 84-87.

163. Editorial, Nov. 14, 1961.

164. The UN's single enumerator law.

165. Quebec Legislative Assembly— *VOTES & PROCEEDINGS*, 26th Legislature, 3rd Session, No.1, Jan.9, 1962, p. 12.

166. Feb. 14, 1962

167. *VOTES & PROCEEDINGS*, No. 93, July 6, 1962, pp.817-8.

168. L. Massicotte, "Une Reforme inachevée: Les règles du jeu electoral", *RECHERCHES SOCIOGRAPHIQUES*, XXV:1, 1984, 43-82.

171. *THE MONTREAL STAR*, March 24, 1966.

172. H.M. Angell, RCOEE, 316.

173. *THE MONTREAL STAR,* March 24, 1966, p.70.

174. "Quebec Changes Governments", *FOREIGN AFFAIRS*, 45:1, Oct. 1966, 148.

175. V. Lemiex, "Les influences imprévus de la loi et de la carte électorales nouvelles", *SOCIALISME*, Nos. 9-10, oct.--dec. 1966. Louis Massicotte, "Une reforme inachevée..."

CHAPTER 4

176. RSQ, c. F--2, 1977.

CHAPTER 5

177. G. Praser, *PQ: RENE LEVESQUE & THE PARTI QUEBECOIS IN POWER* Toronto: Macmillan, 1984 pp. 114-16.

178. "Une reforme inachevée" p.20 Translation by H.M. Angell.

179. Ibid, 10.

180. The former $3,000 aggregate donation per year was amended in April 1989 to allow $3,000 per party per year. This has been the only financing change to Bill 2 since its enactment.

181. H.M. Angell, "Le Financement des partis politiques provinciaux québecois" Chapter 2 in *PERSONNEL ET PARTIS POLITIQUES AU QUÉBEC* (Montreal, Boréal Express, 1982) V. Lemieux (Ed) Table I.

182. Angell, "The Decline of The PQ: A Mass Party, the Polls & Political Financing." Paper presented to the XIIIth IPSA Congress, Paris, 1985, Table II. PQ expenditures were over 90% (92.2%) of permitted, for the second time, in the 1994 election.

183. Massicotte, 18.

184. For a different interpretation see Alain Albert, "La participation politique: Les contributions monetaires aux partis politiques québecois" CJPS, XIV, June 1981, 405.

185. Ibid, 19-20.

186. Angell, "Duverger, Epstein & The Problem of the Mass Party: The Case of the PQ", CJPS XX:2 (June 1987).

187. John Parisella, quoted in *THE GLOBE & MAIL*, November 25, 1987, p. A8. See Angell "The Quebec Liberal Party as a Mass/Cadre Party". Presented to the "Democracy with Justice" conference, Carleton University, February 10, 1990, 12-13. See also infra Chapter 7.

188. See, for further argument, Chapter 7, infra. based on Angell, "The QLP as a Mass/Cadre Party", February 1990.

CHAPTER 6

189. Duverger, *POLITICAL PARTIES*, 1963, 63-71
190. For example, both the federal Liberal and Federal Progressive Conservative parties have reported receiving a donation of $50,000 from the Canadian Pacific corporation in recent years.
191. Although M.B. Stein, "The Structure & Function of The Finances of The Ralliement des Créditistes" in *STUDIES IN CANADIAN PARTY FINANCE* (Ottawa: Queen's Printer, 1966) claims that the Ralliement was the first true mass party in Canada. However, the fact that, as soon as there were a few "bourgeois" members, its executive designed the Club des cents, shows that the Créditistes were a mass party, only "faute de mieux", and not at all by conviction or necessity, as was the PQ at its foundation, as have been most other parties which use a mass financing method.
192. See Vera Murray, *LE PARTI QUÉBECOIS: DE LA FONDATION À LA PRISE DU POUVOIR* (Montreal: Hurtubise, 1976) and Graham Fraser, *PQ: RENE LEVESQUE & THE PARTI QUÉBECOIS IN POWER* (Toronto: Macmillan, 1984).
193. RSQ c. F-2, "An Act to Govern the Financing of Political Parties".
194. (1) "The QLP as a Mass/Cadre Party" for the "Democracy with Justice" conference at Carleton University, February 1990; (2) "Duverger Revisited: The Mass/Cadre Party, for the Political Finance panel of the XVth World Congress of the International Political Science Association, Buenos Aires, July 1991.
195. For more debate on the Quebec law system see H.M. Angell, "Duverger, Epstein & the Problem of the Mass Party; The Case of the PQ", *CJPS* XX:2, (June 1987) 363-78.
196. Angell, "Financing Quebec's Parties: Further Organizational & Financial Decline of the PQ: Buoyancy of the QLP", for the Political Finance panel of the XIVth World Congress of the International Political Science Association, Washington DC, August 1988, p.2.
197. Angell, "The Decline of the PQ: A Mass Party, the Polls & Political Financing," for the Political Finance panel of the XIIIrd World Congress of the International Political Science Association, Paris, July 1985.

196. Angell, "Financing Quebec's Parties: Further Organizational & Financial Decline of the PQ: Buoyancy of the QLP", for the Political Finance panel of the XIVth World Congress of the International Political Science Association, Washington DC, August 1988, p.2.

197. Angell, "The Decline of the PQ: A Mass Party, the Polls & Political Financing," for the Political Finance panel of the XIIIrd World Congress of the International Political Science Association, Paris, July 1985.

198. Statistic supplied by Mme. D. Lajeunesse, QLP HQ, Public Relations, August 4, 1987.

199. In January 1989, the Chairman of the federal Quebec Liberal Caucus, Alfonso Gagliano, recounted how it works in *THE* (Montreal) *GAZETTE*, January 30, 1989, p. A8.

200. Angell, "Le Financement des partis politiques provinciaux québecois," (1982). In English see "Political Finance in Quebec" (1982.)

201. See supra, Chapter 2

202. See, for example, Conrad Black, *DUPLESSIS* (Toronto: McCleland & Stewart, 1977) and Angell, "Political Finance in Quebec".

203. Duverger, 63-71

204. Angell, "The QLP as a Mass/Cadre Party and "Duverger Revisited: The Mass/Cadre Party."

205. Toronto *GLOBE & MAIL*, November 25, 1987, p.A8.

206. A public inquiry showed that a single engineering company contributed $750,000 to the QLP before the 1976 election.

207. In *The* (Montreal) *GAZETTE*, May 3, 1989.

CHAPTER 7

208. *PQ: RENE LEVESQUE & THE PARTI QUÉBECOIS IN POWER* (Toronto, Macmillan, 1984).

BIBLIOGRAPHY

Works by the author:
Harold M. Angell

Quebec Provincial Politics in the 1920's" (1960).

"The Evolution & Application of Quebec's Election Expense Legislation" (1966).

"Le Financement des partis politiques provinciaux au Quebec" (1982).

"Political Finance in Quebec" (1982).

"Decline of the PQ: A Mass Party, the Polls & Political Financing" (1985).

"Duverger, Epstein & the Problem of the Mass Party: The Case of the PQ" (1987).

"Financing Quebec's Parties: Further Organizational & Financial Decline of the PQ: Buoyancy of the QLP" (1988).

"The Quebec Electoral System, 1968 & 1988.

Party & Candidate Spending in the Quebec General Election of April 1981" (unpublished).

"Issue Paper for the Royal Commission on Electoral Reform & Party Financing: Provincial Party Financing in Quebec, 1963 to date" (1990).

"The Quebec Liberal Party as a Mass/Cadre Party" (1990).

"Duverger Revisited: The Mass/Cadre Party" (1991).

Other works consulted

Albert, Alain, "La participation politique: Les contributions monetaires aux partis politiques québecois" (1981).

Behiels, Michael D. PRELUDE T0 THE QUIET REVOLUTION: LIBERALISM VERSUS NEO-NATIONALISM (1985).

Bergeron, Gerard, "Les partis liberaux".

Bergeron, Léandre, A HISTORY OF QUEBEC: A PATRIOTE'S HANDBOOK (1971).

Black, Conrad, DUPLESSIS (1977).

Brunet, Michel, LA PRESENCE ANGLAISE ET LES CANADIENS.

Comeau, P-A. "La transformation du PLQ" (1965).

Dawson, MacGregor, THE GOVERNMENT OF CANADA, 5th edition (1970).

Durocher, M. Le long règne de Duplessis: Un essai d'explication (1971).

Duverger, Maurice, POLITICAL PARTIES, 3rd edition (1963).

Epstein, Leon D. POLITICAL PARTIES IN WESTERN DEMOCRACIES (1967).

Fraser, Graham, PQ: RENE LEVESQUE & THE PARTI QUEBECOIS IN POWER (1984).

Guindon, Hubert, "Social Unrest, Social Class & Quebec's Bureaucratic Revolution (1964).

Hamelin, J. & L. LES MOEURS ELECTORALES AU QUEBEC (1962).

Key, V.O. AMERICAN STATE POLITICS (1956).

Key, V.O. SOUTHERN POLITICS (1949).

Heintzman, R. "Image & Consequences" (1978).

Heintzman, R. "Political Culture of Quebec 1840-1960" (1983).

Landfried, C. "Money & Politics in France" (1989).

Lapalme, Georges-Emile, MEMOIRES, Vol.1 LE VENT DE L'OUBLI, Vol.2, LE PARADIS DE POUVOIR (1979).

Laporte, Pierre, "La machine electorale" (1952).

Lemieux, Vincent, "Les influences de la loi et de la carte électorales nouvelles" (1966).

Mackenzie King, William, DIARY 1935).

Murray, Vera, LE PARTI QUEBECOIS: DE LA FONDATION A LA PRISE DU POUVOIR (1976).

Neatby, B., WILLIAM LYON MACKENZIE KING Vols. 2 & 3. THE LONELY HEIGHTS (1953-77).

Paltiel, Khayyam Z. POLITICAL PARTY FINANCING IN CANADA (1970).

Quinn, Herbert F. THE UNION NATIONALE (1963).

Regehr, T.D. THE BEAUHARNOIS SCANDAL: A STORY OF CANADIAN ENTREPRENEURSHIP & POLITICS (1990).

Regenstreif, Peter, THE DIEFENBAKER INTERLUDE (1965), REPORT OF THE COMMITTEE ON ELECTION EXPENSES & STUDIES IN CANADIAN PARTY FINANCE 1966).

Rumilly, Robert, HISTOIRE DE LA PROVINCE DU QUEBEC, 41 vols. (1940- 69).

Ryan, Claude "Quebec Changes Governments" (1966).

Salvas Commission, purchasing methods of the U.N. (1963).

Schuyler, R.L. & C.C., Weston, British Constitutional History since 1832 (1957).

Stein, M.B., "The Structure & Functions of the Finances of the Ralliement des Créditistes" (1966).

Thomson, Dale C., LOUIS ST. LAURENT: CANADIAN (1967).

Trudeau, P.E., "Some Obstacles to Democracy in Quebec" (1958).

Ward, Norman, ed. A PARTY POLITICIAN: THE MEMOIRS OF CHUBBY POWER (1966).

Wearing, Joseph, The "L" Shaped Party, 1981.

Whitaker, Reginald, THE GOVERNMENT PARTY: ORGANIZING & FINANCING THE LIBERAL PARTY OF CANADA 1930-1958 (1977).